■BEATIFUL THINGS TO MAKE FOR
baby

🐤 Knitting 🐤 Sewing 🐤 Crochet 🐤 Embroidery

METRIC/IMPERIAL CONVERSION CHART

METRIC	INCHES
2mm	1/16
6 mm	1/4
1cm	3/8
2.5 cm	1
5 cm	2
30 cm	12
91 cm	36

ALL ABOUT SIZES

All sewn garments are given in one of two sizes:

0 to 6 months

6 to 12 months

All knitted garments are sized by actual measurements given in both centimetres and inches.

All our patterns are graded so that you can choose a pattern that is just right for you to make.

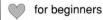 for beginners

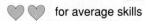 for average skills

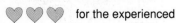 for the experienced

The arrival of a new baby is the most exciting news and what is the first thing we 'crafty' people do when we hear of a new baby expected in the family or among our friends? We rush straight to our box of dog-eared patterns for that special gift to make. Well it's all here — knitting, sewing, crochet and embroidery. There are traditional and modern styles to suit every baby and every knitter or sewer.

Each design is pictured and accompanied by easy to follow instructions. Follow our special hints and tips to ensure a perfect result. There are designs included for babies of all ages from birth to about one year.

EDITORIAL
Craft Editor: Tonia Todman
Managing Editor: Judy Poulos
Editor: Marian Broderick
Editorial Co-ordinator: Margaret Kelly
Assistant Craft Editor: Sally Pereira
Sewing and craft assistance: Martina Oprey,
Yvonne Deacon, Elsie Hamerlok, Natalie Wise,
Ann Cavalho

KNITTING DESIGN
All patterns knitted, crocheted, designed and written
by Sheryl Braden; Sue Morton; Kathy Jarvis and
Wyn McNamara

DESIGN AND PRODUCTION
Nadia Sbisa; Margie Mulray; Chris Hatcher

ILLUSTRATIONS
Greg Gaul

PHOTOGRAPHY
Andrew Elton
Andrew Payne
Cover photography: John Waddy
Cover design: Frank Pithers; Styling: Sally Hirst

PUBLISHER
Philippa Sandall

Family Circle is a registered trademark ® of IPC
Magazines Ltd.
Published by J. B. Fairfax Press by arrangement
with IPC Magazines Ltd.
© J. B. Fairfax Press Pty Ltd, 1990
This book is copyright. Apart from any fair dealing
for the purpose of private study, research, criticism
or review, as permitted under the Copyright Act, no
part may be reproduced by any process without the
written permission of the publisher. Enquiries
should be made in writing to the publisher.

Beautiful Things to Make for Baby
ISBN 1 - 86343 - 032 - 6
Formatted by J.B. Fairfax Press Pty Ltd
Output by Adtype, Sydney
Printed by Toppan Printing Co, Hong Kong
Distributed by J.B. Fairfax Press Ltd

Contents

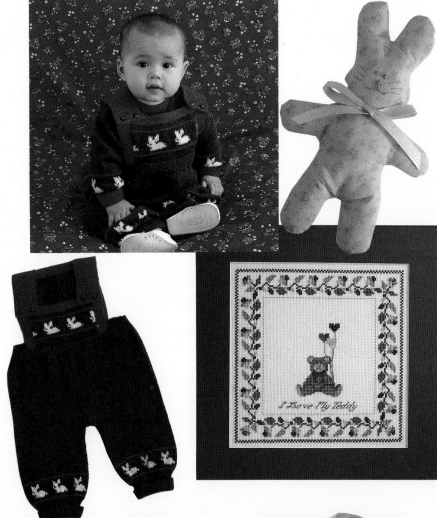

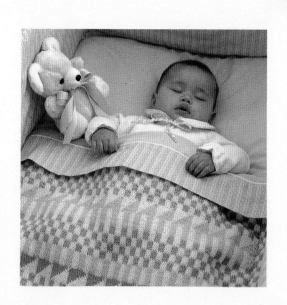

4

Spring Baby

All the colours and freshness of Spring! There are cosy knits to wear on their own or to team with crisp cottons. See how we've spiced up a simple knitted suit with some baby-sized motifs, then repeated the same motifs on the beautiful appliqued cot cover. If you're a whizz with a crochet hook, there's a rug and matching cushions to make, coloured with a touch of primroses.

CROCHET COT COVER AND CUSHIONS

Motif A
Make 10 for Cot Cover and 2 for each Cushion.

Using hook and C3, make 6ch, join with a sl st to form a ring.

1st rnd: 1ch, (3dc, 4ch) 4 times in ring, sl st in first ch at beg.

2nd rnd: 1ch, 1dc in next dc, * 1dc in each of next 2dc, sl st in next 4ch lp, 9ch, sl st in same 4ch lp, 1dc in next dc, rep from * 3 times omitting 1dc in next dc in last rep, sl st in first ch at beg. Fasten off.

3rd rnd: Holding 9ch lp to front, join C2 with a sl st in 4ch sp of 1st rnd, 3ch, (1tr, 2ch, 2tr) in space behind 9ch lp, 1tr in each of next 3dc, * holding 9ch lp to front (2tr, 2ch, 2tr) in 4ch sp of 1st rnd, 1tr in each of next 3dc, rep from * to end, sl st in 3rd ch at beg.

4th rnd: 3ch, 1tr in next tr, * 2tr in next 2ch sp, 1tr in 9ch lp, 9ch, sl st in first of these ch, 1 tr in 9ch lp, 2tr in same 2ch, 1tr in each of next 2tr, 3ch, miss 3tr, 1tr in each of next 2tr, rep from * omitting 1tr in each of next 2tr at end of last rep, using C1 sl st in 3rd ch at beg.

5th rnd: Using C1, 3ch, * 1tr in each of next 3tr, with 9ch lp in front of work (2tr, 2ch, 2tr) around sl st at base of 9ch of 4th rnd, 1tr in each of next 4tr, working in front of 3ch of 4th rnd, 1 dtr in each of next 3tr of 3rd rnd, 1tr in next tr, rep from * omitting 1tr in next tr at end of last rep, sl st in 3rd ch at beg.

6th rnd: 3ch, * 1tr in each of next 5tr, 2tr in next 2ch sp, 1tr in 9ch lp of 4th rnd, 9ch, sl st back into first of these ch, 1tr in same 9ch lp of 4th rnd, 2tr in same 2ch sp of 5th rnd, 1tr in each of next 6tr, 3ch, miss 3 dtr, 1tr in next tr, rep from * omitting 1tr in next tr at end of last rep, using MC sl st in 3rd ch at beg.

7th rnd: Using MC, 3ch, * 1tr in each of next 7tr, with 9ch lp in front of work (2tr, 1ch, 2tr) around sl st at base of 9ch of 6th rnd, 1tr in each of next 8tr, 1 dtr in each of next 3 dtr of 5th rnd, 1tr in next tr, rep from * omitting 1tr in next tr at end of last rep, sl

MEASUREMENTS
Cot Cover: approx 117 cm x 71 cm (including border)
Cushions: approx 31 cm x 31 cm (including border)

MATERIALS
Cleckheaton Babysoft 4 ply (25 g) balls (or other suitable 4 ply): 16 balls of main colour (MC), and 6 balls each of 1st, 2nd and 3rd contrasts (C1, C2 and C3) for Cot Cover; 3 balls of MC and 1 ball each of 1st, 2nd and 3rd contrasts for 2 Cushions; a 3 mm (No. 10-11) crochet hook or the required size to give correct tension; filling for Cushions.

TENSION
23 tr and 12 rows to 10 cm, using a 3 mm hook.

It is important to knit a tension square and to work to the stated tension in order to obtain the required measurements. If your square is bigger use finer needles. If your square is smaller use thicker needles.

st in 3rd ch at beg.

8th rnd: 1ch, * 1dc in each st to corner, 1ch sp, 1ch, 1dc in 9ch lp of 6th rnd, 1ch, rep from * to end, sl st in 1ch at beg. Fasten off.

Motif B
Make 10 for Cot Cover and 2 for each Cushion.

Work as for Motif A, using C1 in place of C3, C3 in place of C2, and C2 in place of C1.

Motif C
Make 10 for Cot Cover and 1 for each Cushion.

Work as for Motif A, using C1 in place of C2, and C2 in place of C1.

Motif D
Make 10 for Cot Cover and 1 for each Cushion.

Work as for Motif A, using C2 in place of C3, and C3 in place of C2.

Motif E
Make 10 for Cot Cover and 1 for each Cushion.

Work as for Motif A, using C1 in place of C2, C3 in place of C1, and C2 in place of C3.

Motif F
Make 10 for Cot Cover and 1 for each Cushion.

Work as for Motif A, using C1 in place of C3, and C3 in place of C1.

TO MAKE UP
Using a flat seam, join motifs together as indicated in diagrams below.

For Cushions:
With wrong sides together, using MC, work dc around three edges to join pieces – noting to work 3dc in each corner dc, and

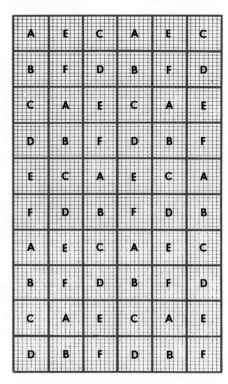

to have a multiple of 10 plus 1tr between corners. Fill Cushions and close remaining edge.

For Cot Cover:
Using MC, work 1 round of dc evenly around all edges – noting to work 3dc in each corner dc, and to have a multiple of 10 plus 1tr between corners. Sl st in first dc at beg. Fasten off.

Border (for Cot Cover and Cushions):
Using MC, beg at one corner —

1st rnd: 1ch, (1dc in corner dc, 5ch, miss 3dc, * 1dc in each of next 7dc, 5ch, miss 3dc, rep from * to next corner dc) 4 times, sl st in 1st dc at beg.

2nd rnd: 4ch, ** into the 5ch lp work a "leaf" thus *, (yoh) twice, insert hook under lp, yoh, and draw lp through, (yoh and draw through 2 lps on hook) twice*, you thus have 2 lps remaining on hook, rep from * to * twice more, you thus have 4 lps on hook, yoh, and draw through 3 lps on hook, yoh and draw through rem 2 lps on hook to complete the "leaf" (3ch, work a 2nd "leaf", 5ch, work a 3rd "leaf", 3ch, work a 4th "leaf") all into same 5ch lp as first "leaf" **, rep from ** to ** in each 5ch lp, noting to miss the dc between each lp, sl st in 4ch at beg.

3rd rnd: 4ch, rep from ** to ** of 2nd rnd in each 5ch lp, sl st in 4ch at beg. Fasten off.

EASY PICTURE QUILT

MATERIALS
☐ 1.3 m of 115 cm wide green cotton fabric for backing and three squares; 30 cm of 115 cm wide yellow cotton fabric for three squares; scraps of fabric for appliques and borders
☐ piece of wadding (batting), 75 cm x 105 cm
☐ fusible interfacing for motifs

PATTERN
NOTE: Some machine quilters may wish to add length to cut pieces to allow for fabric movement during sewing.

1 cm seams allowed. Sew all seams with

right sides facing.

Cut green fabric 72 cm x 102 cm for quilt back; wadding 72 cm x 102 cm; two pieces green fabric 6 cm x 75 cm for top and bottom borders and two pieces 105 cm x 6 cm for side borders. Cut three squares each of green and yellow fabric each 28 cm x 28 cm; strips of white fabric - two 70 cm x 8 cm; two 88 cm x 8 cm; one 88 cm x 6 cm; four 28 cm x 6 cm.

Draw and cut out the following shapes for applique patterns: three rectangles each 8 cm x 15 cm for houses; three triangles 19 cm x 12 cm x 12 cm for roof sections; three boats where keel is 9 cm long, deck is 17 cm long and 5 cm high with sloped sides as shown; three triangles each 16 cm x 13 cm x 13 cm for sails; small window, door and chimney shapes.

1   Interface all applique pieces. Tack pieces onto squares as shown. Stitch them into place, using a narrow zigzag stitch, making three houses and three boats. Trim excess fabric away close to stitching. Stitch around applique pieces again, using wider satin stitch, covering raw edges and previous stitching.

2   Sew 28 cm white strip to lower edge of green square with boat. Sew yellow square with house to lower edge of white strip. Sew second 28 cm white strip to lower edge of yellow square. Sew green square with boat to lower edge of white strip.

3   Make up other half of quilt top in same manner, alternating green with yellow as shown. Join two halves of quilt, sewing 88 cm x 6 cm white strip in between. Press all seams flat.

4   Sew two 88 cm x 8 cm white strips down both sides of quilt top. Sew two 70 cm x 8 cm white strips across top and bottom edges.

5   Tack quilt top to wadding around edges, noting that wadding extends 1 cm beyond quilt all around.

6   Place quilt top onto green backing with wrong sides together. Tack.

7   Sew top, side and bottom border strips into place on right side of quilt top. Turn strips to quilt back. Turn in all raw edges and handsew into place.

8   Complete quilt by stitching through all thicknesses, around edges of all squares, white strips and green borders.

BABY'S ALL-IN-ONE

BACK RIGHT LEG (beg at ankles)
** Using 2.25 mm needles and MC, cast on 25 sts.
1st row: K2, * P1, K1, rep from * to last st, K1.
2nd row: K1, * P1, K1, rep from * to end.
Rep 1st and 2nd rows once.
Using C, rep 1st and 2nd rows once.
Using MC, rep 1st and 2nd rows once, then 1st row once.
Next row: (Inc in next st, rib 1) 5(2) times, inc in each of next 5(17) sts, (rib 1, inc in next st) 5(2) times. 40(46) sts.
Change to 3 mm needles.
Using MC, work 18 rows st st
(1 row K, 1 row P).
Using C, work 4 rows garter st (every row knit).
Last 22 rows form patt.
Cont. in patt until work measures 14.5(16.5) cm from beg, working last row on wrong side. **
Keeping patt correct, inc one st at end of every row 5 times, then in foll alt row. 46(52) sts. Break off yarn, leave sts on a stitch holder.

BACK LEFT LEG
Work as from ** to **.
Keeping patt correct, inc one st at beg of every row 5 times, then in foll alt row. 46(52) sts.
Next row: Patt across 46(52) sts, then patt across 46(52) sts on stitch holder. 92(104) sts.

Shape crotch
Keeping patt correct:
Next row: Patt 44(50), (patt 2tog) twice, patt 44(50).
Work 1 row.
Next row: Patt 43(49), (patt 2tog) twice, patt 43(49).
Work 1 row.
Next row: Patt 42(48), (patt 2tog) twice, patt 42(48).
Cont dec in this manner in foll alt rows until 78(90) sts rem, then in foll 4th rows until 74(86) sts rem. ***
Keeping patt correct, cont until work measures approx 40(44) cm from beg of ankle, ending with 4 rows C.
Tie coloured threads at each end of last

MEASUREMENTS

To fit underarm			
	cm	41	46
	ins	16	18
Actual measurement			
	cm	46	51
Length (underarm to ankle) approx			
	cm	42	46.5
Sleeve seam	cm	13	15

MATERIALS
Cleckheaton Babysoft 3 ply (25 g) balls (or other suitable 3 ply): 3(4) balls of main colour (MC), 1 ball of contrast (C); 1 pair each 3 mm (No. 11) and 2.25 mm (No. 13) knitting needles or the required size to give correct tension; a stitch holder; 5 (6) buttons.

TENSION
This garment has been designed at a tension of 32 sts to 10 cm over st st, using 3 mm needles.
It is important to knit a tension square and to work to the stated tension in order to obtain the required measurements. If your square is bigger use finer needles. If your square is smaller use thicker needles.

row to denote armholes.
Using MC only, work 42(46) rows st st.
Shape shoulders
Cast off 8(10) sts at beg of next 4 rows, then 8(9) sts at beg of foll 2 rows. Leave rem 26(28) sts on a stitch holder.

FRONT
Work as given for Back to ***.
Work 1 row.
Divide for front opening
Keeping patt correct:
Next row: Patt 34(40), cast off next 6 sts, patt 34(40).
Cont on last 34(40) sts until work measures same as Back to coloured threads and ending with 4 rows C.
Tie coloured thread at beg of last row to denote armhole.
Using MC only, work 24(28) rows st st.
Shape neck
Cast off 5 sts at beg of next row.
Dec one st at neck edge in foll alt rows until 24(29) sts rem.
Work 8(6) rows.
Shape shoulder
Cast off 8(10) sts at beg of next row and foll alt row.
Work 1 row.
Cast off.
Join yarn to rem sts and complete to

correspond with other side, noting to tie coloured thread at end of last row and work one row more before shaping neck.

SLEEVES

Using 2.25 mm needles and MC, cast on 41(45) sts.

Work 10 rows rib and stripes as for lower band of Back, inc 12 sts evenly across last row. 53(57) sts.

Change to 3 mm needles.

Cont in st st, inc one st at each end of 3rd and foll 4th row/s until there are 59(61) sts, then in foll 6th rows until there are 65(71) sts. Cont without shaping, until side edge measures 13(15) cm from beg, ending with a purl row.

Shape top

Cast off 8(9) sts at beg of next 6 rows. Cast off rem sts.

RIGHT FRONT BAND

Using back stitch, join shoulder seams. With right side facing, using 2.25 mm needles and MC, knit up 73(85) sts evenly along front edge to neck shaping.

Work 3 rows rib as for lower band of Back, beg with a 2nd row.

Using C:

Next row: Rib 7, * yfwd, work 2tog, rib 15(14), rep from * 2(3) times more, yfwd, work 2tog, rib 13(12). 4(5) buttonholes.

Work 1 row.

Using MC, work 4 rows rib.

Cast off loosely in rib.

LEFT FRONT BAND

Work as for Right Front Band, omitting buttonholes.

NECKBAND

With right side facing, using 2.25 mm needles and MC, knit up 63(65) sts evenly along neck edge and side edge of front bands (including sts from stitch holder).

Work 3 rows rib as for lower band of Back, beg with a 2nd row.

Using C:

Next row: Rib 3, yfwd, work 2tog, rib to end.

Work 1 row.

Using MC, work 4 rows.

Cast off loosely in rib.

TO MAKE UP

Using back stitch, sew in sleeves between coloured threads, placing centre of sleeves to shoulder seams. Join side, sleeve and leg seams. Sew front bands in position overlapping at centre where sts were cast off. Sew on buttons.

Size 16 Back rib 12 rows 3 cms.

GREEN KNIT CARDIGAN

BACK

Using 2.25 mm needles, cast on 71(79,85,93) sts.

1st row: K2, *P1, K1, rep from * to last st, K1.

2nd row: K1, *P1, K1, rep from * to end.

Rep 1st and 2nd rows until band measures 3(3,3,4) cm from beg, ending with a 2nd row.

Change to 3 mm needles.

Work 4 rows st st (1 row K, 1 row P).

5th row: K5(3,6,4), *yfwd, sl1, K1, psso, K4, rep from * to last 0(4,1,5) st/s, (yfwd, sl1, K1, psso) 0(1,0,1) time/s, K0 (2,1,3).

6th row: Purl.

7th row: K3(1,4,2), *K2tog, yfwd, K1, yfwd, sl1, K1, psso, K1, rep from * to last 2(0,3,1) st/s, K2(0,3,1).

Work 5 rows st st, beg with a purl row.

13th row: K2(6,3,1), * yfwd, sl1, K1, psso, K4, rep from * to last 3(1,4,2) sts, (yfwd, sl1, K1, psso) 1(0,1,1) time/s, K1(1,2,0).

14th row: Purl.

15th row: K3(4,1,2), (yfwd, sl1, K1, psso, K1) 1(0,0,1) time/s, *K2tog, yfwd, K1, yfwd, sl1, K1, psso, K1, rep from * to last 5(3,0,4) sts, (K2tog, yfwd), 1(0,0,1) time/s, K3(3,0,2).

MEASUREMENTS

To fit underarm	cm	41	46	51	56
	ins	16	18	20	22
Actual measurement					
	cm	44	50	55	60
Length to back neck approx					
	cm	23	26	30	34
Sleeve seam	cm	14	17	20	24

MATERIALS

Cleckheaton Babysoft 3 ply (25 g) balls (or other suitable 3 ply): 2(2,3,4 balls); 1 pair each 3 mm (No. 11) and 2.25 mm (No. 13) knitting needles or the required size to give correct tension; 8 small buttons; 4 press studs.

TENSION

This garment has been designed at a tension of 32 sts to 10 cm over st st, using 3 mm needles.

It is important to knit a tension square and to work to the stated tension in order to obtain the required measurements. If your square is bigger use finer needles. If your square is smaller use thicker needles.

16th row: Purl.

Last 16 rows form patt.

Work a further 68(80,96,108) rows patt.

Shape shoulders

Keeping patt correct, cast off 11(13,14,15) sts at beg of next 2 rows, then 12(13,14,16) sts at beg of foll 2 rows.

Cast off 25(27,29,31) sts.

LEFT FRONT

Using 2.25 mm needles, cast on 51(57,63,69) sts.

Work in rib as given for lower band of Back, until band measures 3(3,3,4) cm from beg, ending with a 2nd row and inc 0(0,1,1) st/s in centre of last row. 51(57,64,70) sts.

Change to 3 mm needles. **

Work 4 rows st st.

5th row: K5(3,6,4), *yfwd, sl1, K1, psso, K4, rep from * to last 4(0,4,0) sts, (yfwd, sl1, K1, psso) 1(0,1,0) time/s, K2(0,2,0).

6th row: Purl.

7th row: K3(1,4,2), * K2tog, yfwd, K1, yfwd, sl1, K1, psso, K1, rep from * to last 0(2,0,2) sts, K0(2,0,2).

Work 5 rows st st (beg with a purl row).
13th row: K2(6,3,1), *yfwd, sl1, K1, psso, K4, rep from * to last 1(3,1,3) st/s, (yfwd, sl1, K1, psso) 0(1,0,1) time/s K1.
14th row: Purl.
15th row: K3(4,1,2), (yfwd, sl1, K1, psso, K1), 1(0,0,1) time/s, *K2tog, yfwd, K1, yfwd, sl1, K1, psso, K1, rep from * to last 3(5,3,5) sts, K2tog, yfwd, K1, (yfwd, sl1, K1, psso), 0(1,0,1) time/s.
16th row: Purl.
Last 16 rows form patt.
Keeping patt correct, dec one st at end of next and foll alt rows until 28(33,39,43) sts rem, then in foll 4th rows until 23(26,28,31) sts rem.
Work 3(5,3,7) rows.
Shape shoulder
Keeping patt correct, cast off 11(13,14,15) sts at beg of next row.
Work 1 row.
Cast off.
RIGHT FRONT
Work as for Left Front to **.
Work 4 rows st st.
5th row: K3(5,3,5), *yfwd, sl1, K1, psso, K4, rep from * to last 0(4,1,5) st/s, (yfwd, sl1, K1, psso) 0(1,0,1) time/s, K0(2,1,3).
6th row: Purl.
7th row: K1(3,1,3), *K2tog, yfwd, K1, yfwd, sl1, K1, psso, K1, rep from * to last 2(0,3,1) st/s, K2(0,3,1).

Work 5 rows st st, beg with a purl row.
13th row: K6(2,6,2), *yfwd, sl1, K1, psso, K4, rep from * to last 3(1,4,2) st/s, (yfwd, sl1, K1, psso) 1(0,1,1) time/s, K1(1,2,0).
14th row: Purl.
15th row: (K1, yfwd, sl1, K1, psso, K1) 1,(0,1,0) time/s, * K2tog, yfwd, K1, yfwd, sl1, K1, psso, K1, rep from * to last 5(3,0,4) sts, (K2tog, yfwd) 1(0,0,1) time/s, K3(3,0,2).
16th row: Purl.
Last 16 rows form patt.
Cont in patt and complete to correspond with Left Front, reversing shapings and working 1 row more before shaping shoulder.
SLEEVES
Using 2.25 mm needles, cast on 41(41,43,43) sts.
Work in rib as given for lower band of Back, until band measures 3 cm from beg, ending with a 2nd row and inc 8(8,6,6) sts evenly across last row. 49 sts.
Change to 3 mm needles.
Work in patt as given for Back, foll instructions as given for "2nd size" AT SAME TIME inc one st at each end of 7th and foll 4th(4th,all,4th) row/s until there are 59(65,53,75) sts, then in foll 6th(6th,4th,6th) row/s until there are 61(67,73,79) sts.
Cont without shaping until side edge

measures 14(17,20,24) cm from beg, ending with a purl row.
Shape top
Keeping patt correct, cast off 5(5,6,6) sts at beg of next 8 rows.
Cast off rem sts.
FRONT BAND
Using back stitch, join shoulder seams.
Using 2.25 mm needles, cast on 9 sts.
1st row: K2,(P1,K1) 3 times, K1.
2nd row: K1,(P1,K1) 4 times.
Rep 1st and 2nd rows once.
5th row: Rib 3, yfwd, K2tog, rib 4.
Work 7 rows rib.
Rep last 8 rows twice, then 5th row once.
4 buttonholes.
Cont in rib without further buttonholes until band is long enough to fit (slightly stretched) evenly along fronts and across back of neck.
Cast off loosely in rib.

TO MAKE UP
Using back stitch, sew in sleeves placing centre of sleeves to shoulder seams. Join side and sleeve seams.
Sew front band in position, placing buttonholes to right front. Overlap fronts, sew on buttons to correspond with buttonholes. Sew 4 more buttons onto Right Front matching buttons. Sew press studs underneath buttons to fasten.

GREEN FLORAL PANTS

SIZE: 6 to 12 months

MATERIALS
☐ 50 cm of 115 cm wide cotton
☐ elastic to fit

PATTERN
Pattern outline ▬ ▬ ▬ ▬ ▬ ▬ ▬
20 front pants (cut 2); 20 back pants (cut 2); 20a leg facings (cut 2)
Using pattern for overalls, cut out pattern pieces as directed, omitting bib and straps. Trace leg facings as separate pieces from legs. 1 cm seams allowed. Join all pieces together with right sides facing.
1   Sew all crotch seams, noting that there are no side seams. Sew inside leg seams.

2 parts, 4 rows.

Green Knit Cardigan, Green Floral Pants, Picture Knit Jumper and Pants

2 Sew side seams of facings. Place facings around ends of legs, with right sides together, raw edges even and seams matching. Sew around ends of legs. Turn facings to inside, turn under raw edge and stitch down. Fold cuffs to right side.

3 Turn raw edge at waist to inside, forming casing. Stitch, leaving opening for inserting elastic. Insert elastic, adjust length and join ends. Close opening by hand.

PICTURE KNIT JUMPER AND PANTS

NOTE: When changing colours in centre of row, twist the colour to be used underneath and to the right of colour just used, making sure both yarns are worked firmly at joins. Always change colours on wrong side of work so colour change does not show on right side. Use a separate ball of yarn for each section of colour. We suggest using bobbins. Wind a quantity of yarn around bobbin and place end through slot to hold. Unwind only enough yarn to knit required sts, then place yarn in slot, keeping bobbin close to work.

JUMPER
BACK
Using 2.25 mm needles and C3, cast on 75(83,91) sts.

1st row: K2, * P1, K1, rep from * to last st, K1.

2nd row: K1, * P1, K1, rep from * to end.
Rep 1st and 2nd rows until band measures 2 cm from beg, ending with a 2nd row, inc one st at end of last row. 76(84,92) sts.
Change to 3 mm needles.
Work rows 1 to 73 inclusive from Graph.
Next row: P38(42,46) MC, P38(42,46) C1.
Next row: K38(42,46) C1, K38(42,46) MC.
Last 2 rows form patt. **
Work 19(23,31) rows patt.
Shape back neck
Keeping patt correct:
Next row: Patt 22(24,27), turn.
Dec one st at neck edge in every row until 19(21,24) sts rem.
Shape shoulder
Cast off 6(7,8) sts at beg of next row and foll alt row.

MEASUREMENTS

To fit underarm	cm	41	46	51
	ins	16	18	20
Jumper actual measurement				
	cm	46	51	56
Length to back neck approx				
	cm	25	27	29
Sleeve seam	cm	15	18	21
Pants outside leg length approx				
	cm	25	28	31

MATERIALS

Cleckheaton Babysoft 3 ply (25 g) balls (or other suitable 3 ply): 1(2,3) ball/s main colour (MC — Pink), 1(2,3) ball/s first Contrast (C1 — Blue), 1 ball each of 2nd and 3rd Contrast (C2 — Yellow), (C3 — Green) for Jumper; 3(3,4) balls of MC, 1 ball of C1, C2 and C3 for Pants; 1 pair each 3 mm (No. 11) and 2.25 mm (No. 13) knitting needles or the required size to give correct tension; 2 stitch holders; bobbins; 3 buttons for Jumper; length of round elastic for Pants.

TENSION

These garments have been designed at a tension of 32 sts to 10 cm over st st, using 3 mm needles

It is important to knit a tension square and to work to the stated tension in order to obtain the required measurements. If your square is bigger use finer needles. If your square is smaller use thicker needles.

Work 1 row.
Cast off.
Slip next 32(36,38) sts on a stitch holder and leave.
Join yarn to rem sts and patt to end.
Complete to correspond with other side of neck.
FRONT
Work as for Back to **.
Work 1(3,9) row/s.
Shape neck
Keeping patt correct:
Next row: Patt 28(31,35), turn.
*** Dec one st at neck edge in every row until 19(21,24) sts rem.
Work 4(5,6) rows. ***
Shape shoulder
Complete as for Back Shoulder shaping.
Slip next 20(22,22) sts on a stitch holder and leave.
Join yarn to rem sts and patt to end.
Rep from *** to ***.
Work 9 rows.
Shape shoulder
Complete as for other shoulder.
LEFT SLEEVE
Using 2.25 mm needles and C3, cast on 41(45,49) sts.
Cont in rib as for lower band of Back, until band measures 2 cm from beg, ending with a 2nd row and inc 11 sts evenly across last row. 52(56,60) sts.
Change to 3 mm needles.
Using MC, cont in st st (1 row K, 1 row P), inc one st at each end of 5th and foll 6th(6th,8th) row/s until there are 60(60,74) sts, then in foll 8th(8th,10th) row/s until

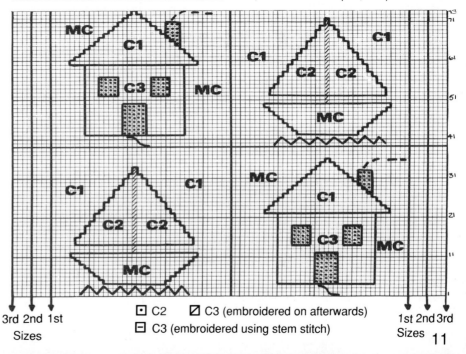

3rd 2nd 1st
Sizes

☐ C2   ☑ C3 (embroidered on afterwards)
☐ C3 (embroidered using stem stitch)

1st 2nd 3rd
Sizes   **11**

there are 64(70,76) sts.

Cont without shaping until side edge measures 15(18,21) cm from beg, ending with a purl row.

Shape top
Cast off 8(9,10) sts at beg of next 6 rows.
Cast off rem sts.

RIGHT SLEEVE
Work as for Left Sleeve, using C1 in place of MC after needle change.

NECKBAND
Using back stitch, join right shoulder seam. With right side facing, using 2.25 mm needles and C3, beg at left shoulder and knit up 103(113,119) sts, evenly around neck edge (including sts from holders).
Cont in rib as for lower band of Back, beg with a 2nd row, until neckband measures 2 cm from beg, ending with a 2nd row.
Cast off loosely in rib.

LEFT FRONT SHOULDER BAND
With right side facing, using 2.25 mm needles and C3, knit up 19(21,23) sts evenly along left front shoulder edge.
Work 3 rows rib as for lower band of Back, beg with a 2nd row.

Next row: Rib 2(3,4), (cast off 2 sts, rib 4) twice, cast off 2 sts, rib 3(4,5).

Next row: Rib 3(4,5), (cast on 2 sts, rib 4) twice, cast on 2 sts, rib 2(3,4). 3 button-holes.
Work 4 rows rib.
Cast off.

LEFT BACK SHOULDER BAND
Work as for Left Front Shoulder Band omitting buttonholes.

TO MAKE UP
Overlap Front Shoulder Band over Back Shoulder Band, and slipstitch in position at armhole edge. Using back stitch, sew in sleeves, placing centre of sleeves to shoulder seams. Join side and sleeve seams. Sew on buttons.

LEGGINGS

RIGHT LEG (beg at waist)
Using 2.25 mm needles and MC, cast on 87(91,95) sts.

1st row: K2, * P1, K1, rep from * to last st, K1.

2nd row: K1, * P1, K1, rep from * to end.
Rep 1st and 2nd rows 4 times, inc one st in centre of last row. 88(92,96) sts.
Change to 3 mm needles.
Work 2 rows st st.

Shape back
Note: When turning, bring yarn to front of work, slip next stitch on to right hand needle, yarn back, slip stitch back onto left hand needle, then turn and proceed as instructed.
This avoids a hole in work. ****

1st row: K12(14,16), turn.
2nd and alt rows: Purl.
3rd row: K19(21,23), turn.
5th row: K26(28,30), turn.
7th row: K33(35,37), turn.
Cont turning in this manner, working 7 more sts in alt rows until the row "K75(77,79), turn" has been worked.
Next row: Purl across all sts.

***** cont in st st, inc one st at each end of 9th row and foll 12th(14th,16th) rows until there are 94(98,102) sts.
Cont until shorter edge measures 16(17,19) cm from beg, ending with a purl row.
Tie a coloured thread at end of last row.

Shape leg
Dec 1 st at each end of next row and foll alt rows until 68(70,72) sts rem.
Work 28(34,40) rows.

Next row: P3(4,5), * P2tog, rep from * to last 3(4,5) sts, P3(4,5). 37(39,41) sts.
Using C3,

Next row: Knit
Work 7 rows rib as for waist, beg with a 2nd row.
Cast off loosely in rib.

LEFT LEG (beg at waist)
Work as for Right Leg to ****.

1st and alt rows: Knit
2nd row: P12(14,16), turn.
4th row: P19(21,23), turn.
6th row: P26(28,30), turn.
8th row: P33(35,37), turn.
Cont turning in this manner, working 7 sts more in alt rows until the row "P75(77,79), turn" has been worked.
Work as for Right Leg from ***** to end.

TO MAKE UP
Using back stitch, join Back, Front and Leg seams. Thread round elastic through 1st, 5th and 9th rows of rib at waist.

♡ HINT ♡

Baby's knitwear needs to be laundered so often that it's important to wash with care. As a rule of thumb, it is best to follow the washing instruction printed on the ball band of your yarn. If this is not possible it is best to wash delicate knits by hand in lukewarm water using pure soap or a soap powder especially formulated for knits.

KNIT A PICTURE

You can work an artist's magic with your knitting needles and a few balls of coloured yarn. Stripes are the simplest of all colour patterns but it is much easier than you think to knit quite a complicated picture.

Following a graph
Picture patterns are often given in the form of a graph, rather than lengthy written instructions. Each colour is represented by a different symbol on the graph. Work the graph from the bottom up, knitting the odd numbered rows and purling the even numbered ones. If a pattern is to be repeated up the garment sometimes only one graph is given, with the number of repeats indicated. It is important to keep track of where you are when knitting from a graph so you might like to cross out or tick rows already worked.

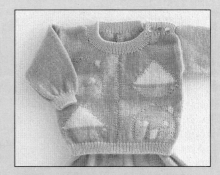

Carrying colours
Colours should be carried across the back of the work only for five stitches. Ideally, each block of colour should be worked from its own ball or bobbin of wool. This prevents "pulling" and bobbins cut down on the tangle of many balls of yarn. To avoid holes in your knitting when changing from one colour to another take care to twist the new colour around the colour just used.

LEMON CROCHET JACKET AND BONNET

JACKET (beg at neck)
Using hook, make 62ch.
1st row: Miss 1ch, 1dc in each ch to end.
61dc.
2nd row: (right side) (1dc, 1ch) in first dc,
* 1ch, miss next 2dc, "Cluster" in next st,
1ch, miss next 2dc, 1tr in next dc, rep from
* to end. 10 "Clusters".
3rd row: (1dc, 1ch) in first tr, 1tr in 1ch sp,
1ch, "Cluster" in 1ch sp of "Cluster" from
previous row, * 1ch, 1tr in next 1ch sp, 1tr
in next tr, 1tr in next 1ch sp, 1ch, "Cluster"
in 1ch sp of "Cluster" from previous row,
rep from * but noting to end with 1ch, 1tr in
next 1ch sp, 1tr in top of turning ch.
4th row: (1dc, 1ch) in first tr, ltr in next tr,
1tr in next 1ch sp, * 1ch, "Cluster" in 1ch sp
of "Cluster" from previous row, 1ch, 1tr in
next ch sp, 1tr in each of next 3tr, 1tr in next
ch sp, rep from * until 1 "Cluster" remains,
1ch "Cluster" in 1ch sp of "Cluster" from
previous row, 1ch, 1tr in next ch sp, 1tr in
next tr, 1tr in top of turning ch.
5th row: (1dc, 1ch) in first tr, 1tr in each of
next 2tr, 1tr in next ch sp, * 1ch, "Cluster"
in 1ch sp of "Cluster" from previous row,
1ch, 1tr in next 1ch sp, 1tr in each of next
5tr, 1tr in next 1ch sp, rep from * until 1
"Cluster" remains, 1ch, "Cluster" in 1ch sp
of "Cluster" from previous row, 1ch, 1tr in
next 1ch sp, 1tr in each of next 2tr, 1tr in
top of turning ch.
Rep 5th row 3 times more, working 2tr
more between "Clusters" and 1tr more at
each end of each row. (There should be
13tr between each "Cluster" and 7tr at
each end upon completion of the 8th row.)
9th row: (1dc, 1ch) in first tr, 1tr in each of
next 6tr, * 1ch, "Cluster" in 1ch sp of
"Cluster" from previous row, 1ch 1tr in
each of next 13tr, rep from * until 1 "Cluster" remains, 1ch, "Cluster" in 1ch sp of
"Cluster" from previous row, 1ch, 1tr in
each of next 6tr, 1tr in top of turning ch.
10th row: (1dc, 1ch) in first tr, miss 1tr,
"Cluster" in next tr, miss 1tr, 1tr in next tr,
miss 1tr, "Cluster" in next tr, 1tr in first tr of
"Cluster", "Cluster" in 1ch sp of "Cluster"

MEASUREMENTS

Jacket		
To fit underarm	cm	46
(about 6 months old) ins		18
Length	cm	24
Sleeve Seam	cm	13
Bonnet		
Fits around face	cm	25

MATERIALS

Cleckheaton Babysoft 4 ply (25 g) balls
(or other suitable 4 ply): 4 balls for
Jacket; 1 ball for Bonnet; a 3 mm (No.
10-11) crochet hook or the required
size to give correct tension.

ABBREVIATION

"Cluster" = (3tr, 1ch, 3tr) all into same
st.

TENSION

4 Clusters and 20 rows to 10 cm over
patt and 23tr and 12 rows to 10 cm.
It is important to knit a tension square
and to work to the stated tension in
order to obtain the required measurements. If your square is bigger use finer
needles. If your square is smaller use
thicker needles.

from previous row, 1tr in last tr of "Cluster",
("Cluster" in next tr, miss 2tr, 1tr in next tr,
miss 2tr) twice, "Cluster" in next tr, 1tr in
first tr of "Cluster", 3tr in 1ch sp of "Cluster"
from previous row, 1ch, miss last 3tr of
"Cluster", (1tr in each of next 13tr, "Cluster" in 1ch sp of "Cluster" from previous
row, miss last 3tr of "Cluster", 1tr in each of
next 13tr) for first Sleeve, 1ch, 3tr in 1ch sp
in centre of next "Cluster", 1tr in last tr of
same "Cluster", ("Cluster" in next tr, miss
2tr, 1tr in next tr, miss 2tr) twice, "Cluster"
in next tr, 1tr in first tr of next "Cluster",
"Cluster" in 1ch sp of "Cluster" from previous row, 1tr in last tr of "Cluster", ("Cluster"
in next tr, miss 2tr, 1tr in next tr, miss 2tr)
twice, "Cluster" in next tr, 1tr in first tr of
next "Cluster", "Cluster" in 1 ch sp of
"Cluster" from previous row, 1 tr in last tr of
"Cluster", ("Cluster in next tr, miss 2tr, 1tr
in next tr, miss 2 tr) twice, "Cluster" in next
tr, 1tr in first tr of next "Cluster", 3tr in 1 ch
sp of "Cluster" from previous row, 1 ch,
miss last 3tr of "Cluster", (1tr in each of
next 13tr, "Cluster" in 1 ch sp of "Cluster"
from previous row, 1tr in each of next 13tr)
for 2nd Sleeve, 1ch, 3tr in 1ch sp of next
"Cluster", 1tr in last tr of same "Cluster",
("Cluster" in next tr, miss 2tr, 1tr in next tr,
miss 2tr) twice, "Cluster" in next tr, 1tr in
first tr of next "Cluster", "Cluster" in 1ch sp
of "Cluster" from previous row, 1tr in last tr
of same "Cluster", "Cluster" in next tr, miss

1tr, 1tr in next tr, miss 1tr, "Cluster" in next tr, miss 1tr, 1tr in top of turning ch.

11th row: (1dc, 1ch) in first tr, ("Cluster" in 1ch sp of "Cluster" from previous row, 1tr in next tr) 6 times, 3tr in next 1ch sp, miss next (13tr, "Cluster", 13tr), 1ch, 3tr in next 1ch sp, miss 3tr, (1tr in next tr, "Cluster" in 1ch sp of "Cluster" from previous row) 11 times, 1tr in next tr, 3tr in next 1ch sp, 1ch, miss next (13tr, "Cluster", 13tr), 1ch, 3tr in next 1ch sp, miss 3tr, (1tr in next tr, "Cluster" in 1ch sp of "Cluster" from previous row) 6 times, 1tr in top of turning ch.

Continue on this section for Back and Fronts as follows:

12th row: (1dc, 1ch) in first tr, ("Cluster" in 1ch sp of "Cluster" from previous row, 1tr in next tr) 6 times, miss 3tr, "Cluster" in next 1ch sp, miss 3tr, (1tr in next tr, "Cluster" in next 1ch sp of "Cluster" from previous row) 11 times, 1tr in next tr, miss 3tr, "Cluster" in next 1ch sp, miss 3tr, (1tr in next tr, "Cluster" in next 1ch sp of "Cluster" from previous row) 6 times, 1tr in top of turning ch.

13th row: (1dc, 1ch) in first tr, * "Cluster" in next 1ch sp of "Cluster" from previous row, 1tr in next tr, rep from * to end, working last tr in top of turning ch.

Rep 13th row 11 times more. DO NOT FASTEN OFF .

Continue up right front edge as follows:

Next row: 2ch, 1dc in first tr, 2dc in each tr to neck edge, 1dc in side of 1st row, 2dc in corner, 1dc in each of next 61dc of foundation row, 2dc in corner, 1dc in side of 1st row, 2dc in each tr to lower edge. Fasten off.

Neck edging

With right side of work facing, rejoin yarn to right neck edge inside 2 corner dc, (1dc, 1ch) in next dc, * miss 2 dc, "Cluster" in next dc, miss 2dc, 1tr in next dc, rep from * to other corner. Fasten off.

SLEEVES (both alike)

With wrong side facing, rejoin yarn with a sl st in 1ch sp at underarm.

1st row: (1dc, 1ch) in 1ch sp, ("Cluster" in next tr, miss 2tr, 1tr in next tr, miss 2tr) twice, "Cluster" in next tr, 1tr in first tr of "Cluster", "Cluster" in 1ch sp of "Cluster" from previous row, 1tr in last tr of "Cluster", ("Cluster" in next tr, miss 2tr, 1tr in next tr, miss 2tr) twice, "Cluster" in next tr, 1tr in 1ch sp at underarm, turn.

2nd row: (1dc, 1ch) in first tr, * "Cluster" in 1ch sp of "Cluster" from previous row, 1tr in next tr, rep from * to end, working last tr

in top of turning ch, then join with a sl st to beg of row.

NOTE: Work sleeve in rounds from this point onwards.

1st rnd: 3ch, * "Cluster" in 1ch sp of "Cluster" from previous row, 1tr in next tr, rep from * to last "Cluster", "Cluster" in 1ch sp of "Cluster" from previous row, sl st in 3ch at beg.

2nd rnd: 3ch, (1tr, 1ch, 1tr) in 1ch sp of "Cluster" from previous round, 1tr in next tr, * "Cluster" in 1ch sp of "Cluster" from previous round, 1 tr in next tr, rep from * to last "Cluster", (1tr, 1ch, 1tr) in 1ch sp of "Cluster" from previous round, sl st in 3ch at beg.

3rd rnd: 3ch, (1tr, 1ch, 1tr) in next 1ch sp, 1tr in next tr, rep from * of 2nd round to last 1ch sp, (1tr, 1ch, 1tr in last 1ch sp, sl st in 3ch at beg.

Rep 3rd round twice.

6th rnd: 3ch, 2tr in same place as sl st, miss (1tr, 1ch, 1tr), 1tr in next tr, * "Cluster" in 1ch sp of "Cluster" from previous round, 1tr in next tr, rep from * 4 times more, miss (1tr, 1ch, 1tr), 3tr between last tr and next tr, 1ch, sl st in 3ch at beg.

7th rnd: 3ch, "Cluster" back into last 1ch sp between beg and end of 6th round, 1tr in next tr, * "Cluster" in 1ch sp of "Cluster" from previous round, 1tr in next tr, rep from * to end, sl st in 3ch at beg.

8th rnd: 3ch, "Cluster" in 1ch sp of "Clus-

ter" from previous round, 1tr in next tr, rep from * to last "Cluster", "Cluster" in 1ch sp of last "Cluster", sl st in 3ch at beg.

Rep 8th round 3 times. Fasten off.

TO MAKE UP

Using a flat seam, join underarm seams. Using 3 strands of yarn (each 264 cm long), make a twisted cord and thread through trebles between "Clusters" at neck edge.

BONNET

Using hook make 13ch.

1st row: Miss 1ch, 1dc in each ch to end.

2nd row: (1dc, 1ch, 1tr) in first dc, 2tr in each of next 10dc, 2tr in top of turning ch. 24 sts.

3rd row: (1dc, 1ch) in first tr, 2tr in next tr, * 1tr in next tr, 2tr in next tr, rep from * to last 2 sts, 1tr in next tr, 1tr in top of turning ch. 35 sts.

4th row: (1dc, 1ch) in first tr, 1tr in next tr, 2tr in next tr, * 1tr in each of next 2tr, 2tr in next tr, rep from * to last 2 sts, 1tr in next tr, 1tr in top of turning ch. 46 sts.

5th row: (1dc, 1ch) in first tr, 1tr in next tr, 2tr in next tr, * 1tr in each of next 3tr, 2tr in next tr, rep from * to last 3 sts, 1tr in each of next 2tr, 1tr in top of turning ch. 57 sts.

6th row: (1dc, 1ch) in first tr, 1tr in each of next 3tr, 2tr in next tr, * 1tr in each of next 15tr, 2tr in next tr, rep from * to last 4 sts, 1tr in each of next 3tr, 1tr in top of turning ch. 61 sts.

Beg patt

1st row: (1dc, 1ch) in first tr, * miss next 2tr, "Cluster" in next tr, miss next 2tr, 1tr in next tr, rep from * to end, working last tr in top of turning ch. 9 "Clusters".

2nd row: (1dc, 1ch) in first tr, * "Cluster" in 1ch sp of "Cluster" from previous row, 1tr in next tr, rep from * to end, working last tr in top of turning ch.

Rep 2nd row 10 times. DO NOT FASTEN OFF.

Thread a length of yarn through row of foundation chain, draw up and fasten off securely. Using back stitch, join back seam for 5 cm from foundation row.

Return to work and work one row of dc evenly along side edges of Bonnet (excluding last row of patt). Fasten off.

TO MAKE UP

Using 3 strands of yarn (each 300 cm long), make a twisted cord and thread through last row of pattern.

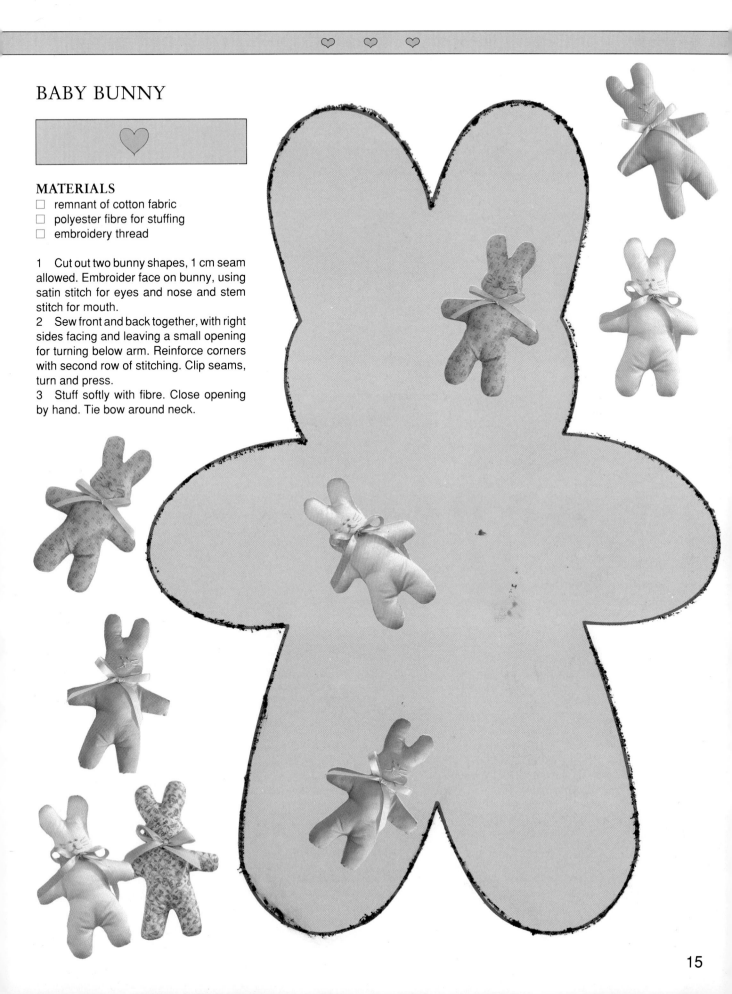

BABY BUNNY

♡

MATERIALS
- ☐ remnant of cotton fabric
- ☐ polyester fibre for stuffing
- ☐ embroidery thread

1   Cut out two bunny shapes, 1 cm seam allowed. Embroider face on bunny, using satin stitch for eyes and nose and stem stitch for mouth.

2   Sew front and back together, with right sides facing and leaving a small opening for turning below arm. Reinforce corners with second row of stitching. Clip seams, turn and press.

3   Stuff softly with fibre. Close opening by hand. Tie bow around neck.

Sunshine

Let the sunshine in with these delicious baby things. Combine traditional styles in these happy colours, decked out in spots, stripes and cheeky ducks. There are frills and flounces for the baby girl and practical overalls, perfect for both boys and girls.

DUCKLING OUTFIT

CARDIGAN

BACK

Using 3 mm needles and MC, cast on 53(61,67) sts.

1st row: K2, *P1, K1, rep from * to last st, K1.

2nd row: K1, *P1, K1, rep from * to end.
Rep 1st and 2nd rows until band measures 3 cm from beg, ending with a 2nd row, inc 7 sts evenly across last row.
60(68,74) sts.
Change to 3.75 mm needles and C1.
Work 4 rows st st (1 row K, 1 row P).
Cont in st st working in stripes of 2 rows C2, 2 rows C1, 2 rows MC and 2 rows C1, until work measures 22(24,27) cm from beg, ending with a purl row.

Shape shoulders

Cast off 7(8,9) sts at beg of next 4 rows, then 7(8,8) sts at beg of foll 2 rows.
Slip rem 18(20,22) sts on a stitch holder and leave.

LEFT FRONT

Using 3 mm needles and MC, cast on 27(31,33) sts.
Cont in rib as for lower band of Back, until band measures 3 cm from beg, ending with a 2nd row, inc 3(3,4) sts evenly across last row. 30(34,37) sts.
Change to 3.75 mm needles and C1.
Work 4 rows st st.
Cont in st st working in stripes as for Back until there are 34(36,40) rows less than back to shoulder shaping.

Shape front slope

Keeping stripes correct, dec one st at end (neck edge) of next and foll 4th (alt, alt) rows 9(3,3) times in all, **2nd and 3rd sizes only** - then in foll 4th rows (7,8) times.
21(24,26) sts.
Work 1(3,3) row/s.

Shape shoulder

Cast off 7(8,9) sts at beg of next and foll alt row.
Work 1 row.
Cast off rem sts.

RIGHT FRONT

Work to correspond with left front.

SLEEVES

Using 3mm needles and MC, cast on 35(35,37) sts.

MEASUREMENTS

To fit underarm	cm	41	46	51
	ins	16	18	20
Cardigan actual measurements				
	cm	48	53	58
Length to back neck				
	cm	22	24	27
Sleeve seam	cm	13	15	18
Jumper actual measurements				
	cm	46	51	56
Length to back neck				
	cm	22	24	27
Sleeve seam	cm	13	15	18
Overalls outside leg seam				
	cm	33	37	44
Bootees				
To fit (age)		Approx 3-7 months		
Length of foot		Approx 8-9 cm		

MATERIALS

Cleckheaton 5 ply Machine Wash (50 g) balls (or other suitable 5 ply): 1(1,2) ball/s Main Colour (MC), 1(1,2) ball/s 1st Contrast (C1 — White), 1 ball 2nd Contrast (C2 — Yellow) for Cardigan; 1(1, 2) ball/s MC, 2(2, 3) balls C1, 1 ball C2, a small quantity of C3 — Red and C4 —Black for Jumper; 2(3, 3) balls of MC, 1 ball each of C1 and C2, a small quantity of C3 and C4 for Overalls; 1 ball MC and 1 ball C1 for Bootees. 1 pair each 3 mm (No. 11) and 3.75 mm (No. 9) knitting needles or the required size to give correct tension; a stitch holder; 4 buttons for Cardigan; 2 stitch holders, bobbins and 6 buttons for Jumper; 2 buttons, bobbins and round elastic for Overalls; 85 cm of 6 mm wide ribbon for Bootees.

TENSION

26 sts to 10 cm over st st, using 3.75 mm needles.
It is important to knit a tension square and to work to the stated tension in order to obtain the required measurements. If your square is bigger use finer needles. If your square is smaller use thicker needles.

Cont in rib as for lower band of Back until band measures 3 cm from beg, ending with a 2nd row and inc 4 sts evenly across last row. 39(39,41) sts.
Change to 3.75 mm needles and C1.
Work 2 rows st st.
Cont in stripes of 2 rows C1, 2 rows C2, 2 rows C1 and 2 rows MC throughout, AT SAME TIME inc one st at each end of next and foll 6th(4th,4th) rows 5(4,6) times in all, **2nd and 3rd sizes only** - then in foll 6th rows 3 times. 49(53,59) sts.
Cont in stripes until side edge measures 13(15,18) cm from beg, working last row on wrong side.

Shape top

Cast off 7(8,9) sts at beg of next 4 rows, then 7(7,8) sts at beg of foll 2 rows. Cast off.

FRONT BAND

Using back stitch, join shoulder seams. With right side facing, using 3 mm needles and MC, knit up 38(44,50) sts evenly along Right Front edge to beg of front slope shaping, knit up 34(36,40) sts evenly along right front slope, knit across 18(20,22) sts from back neck stitch holder, inc one st in centre, knit up 34(36,40) sts evenly along left front slope to where shaping begins, and knit up 38(44,50) sts evenly along Left Front edge. 163(181,203) sts.
Work 1 row rib as for lower band of Back.
Next row: Rib 4,[K2tog, yfwd, rib 8(10,12)] 3 times, K2tog, yfwd, rib to end. 4 button-holes.
Work 3 rows rib.
Cast off loosely in rib.

TO MAKE UP

Using back stitch, sew in sleeves, placing centre of sleeves to shoulder seams. Join side and sleeve seams. Sew on buttons.

JUMPER

BACK

Using 3 mm needles and MC, cast on 53(61,67) sts.

1st row: K2, *P1, K1, rep from * to last st, K1.

2nd row: K1, *P1, K1, rep from * to end.
Rep 1st and 2nd rows until band measures 3 cm from beg, ending with a 2nd row and inc 7 sts evenly across last row.
60(68,74) sts.
Change to 3.75 mm needles.
Work 2 rows st st (1 row K, 1 row P).
NOTE: When working in Fair Isle, do not weave colours but carry colours not in use loosely across on wrong side of work. Always carry colours to ends of rows.
NOTE: When changing colours in centre of row, twist colour to be used under and to right of colour just used, making sure both yarns are worked firmly at joins. Always change colours on wrong side of

work and use separate ball for each section of colour. We suggest using bobbins.

3rd row: *K2C1, K2MC, rep from * to last 0(0,2) sts, K0(0,2) C1.

4th row: P17(21,24) C1, P5C2, P15C1, P5C2, P18(22,25) C1.

Work rows 5 to 22 inclusive from Graph A.

23rd row: *K2MC, K2C1, rep from * to last 0(0,2) sts, K0(0,2) MC.

Using C1, cont in st st until work measures 22(24,27) cm from beg, ending with a purl row.

Tie a coloured thread at each end of last row.

Shape shoulders

Next row: K21(24,26), turn.

** Cast off 2 sts at beg of next and foll alt rows until 3(2,4) sts rem.

Cast off **.

Slip next 18(20,22) sts onto a stitch holder and leave. Join yarn to rem sts and knit to end.

Work 1 row.

Rep from ** to **.

FRONT

Work as for Back until there are 14(14,16) rows less than back to shoulder shaping.

Shape neck

Next row: K25(28,31), turn.

Dec one st at neck edge in alt rows 4(4,5) times. 21(24,26) sts.

Work 6 rows.

Tie a coloured thread at each end of last row.

Shape shoulder

Complete as for back shoulder from ** to **

Slip next 10(12,12) sts onto a stitch holder and leave.

Join yarn to rem sts and complete to cor-

respond with other side, reversing shapings.

SLEEVES

Using 3 mm needles and MC, cast on 33(37,39) sts.

Work in rib as for lower band of Back until band measures 3 cm from beg, working last row on wrong side and inc 4 sts evenly across last row. 37(41,43) sts.

Change to 3.75 mm needles and C1.

Cont in st st, working stripes of 2 rows C1 and 2 rows MC throughout, AT SAME TIME inc one st at each end of 3rd and foll 6th(6th,8th) rows until there are 47(47,55) sts. **2nd size only** – then in foll 8th rows twice. 47(51, 55) sts.

Cont in stripes without shaping until side edge measures 13(15,18) cm from beg, ending with a purl row.

GRAPH A

- ☐ C1
- ☒ C2
- = C3 (embroidered on afterwards)
- ◪ C4 (embroidered on afterwards)

3rd 2nd 1st

Sizes

1st 2nd 3rd

Sizes

Shape top

Cast off 7(7,8) sts at beg of next 4 rows, then 6(8,8) sts at beg of foll 2 rows. Cast off rem sts.

BACK NECKBAND

Using 3 mm needles and MC, with right side facing, knit up 34(36,38) sts evenly along right back shoulder edge, knit across 18(20,22) sts from back neck stitch holder, dec one st in centre, and knit up 34(36,38) sts evenly along left back shoulder edge. 85(91,97) sts.

Next row: Using MC, purl.

Work 2 rows rib, as for lower band of Back.

Next row: Rib 4(4,5), [yfwd, K2tog, rib 8(9,10)] twice, yfwd, K2tog, rib 33(35,35), [yfwd, K2tog, rib 8(9,10)] twice, yfwd, K2tog, rib 4(4,5). 6 buttonholes.

Work 3 rows rib, beg with a 2nd row.

Cast off loosely in rib.

FRONT NECKBAND

Using 3 mm needles and C1, with right side facing, knit up 42(44,46) sts evenly along front left shoulder and side neck edge, knit across 10(12,12) sts from front stitch holder, inc one st in centre and knit up 42(44,46) sts evenly along right shoulder and side neck edge. 95(101,105) sts.

Next row: Using MC, purl.

Work 6 rows rib as for lower band of Back.

Cast off loosely in rib.

TO MAKE UP

With right side of Front facing wrong side of Back, overlap shoulders, matching coloured threads, and slip stitch together at sides. Sew in sleeves, placing centre of sleeve to shoulder seams. Join side and sleeve seams. Sew on buttons. Embroider beaks in C3 as illustrated. Using knitting stitch and C4, embroider eyes on ducks.

OVERALLS

RIGHT LEG (beg at waist)

Using 3 mm needles and MC, cast on 57(63,69) sts.

1st row: K2, *P1, K1, rep from * to last st, K1.

2nd row: K1, *P1, K1, rep from * to end. Rep 1st and 2nd rows once.

Buttonhole row: Rib 20, yfwd, K2tog, rib to end.

Rep 2nd and 1st rows once, then 2nd row once.

Change to 3.75 mm needles.

Work 2 rows st st.

NOTE: When turning, bring yarn to front of

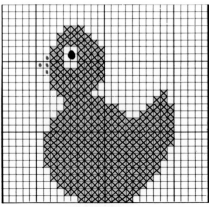

GRAPH B

☐ C1

☒ C2

⊡ C3 (embroidered on afterwards)

work, slip next st onto right hand needle, ybk, slip st back onto left hand needle, then turn and proceed as instructed. This avoids holes in work ***

1st row: K16, turn.

2nd and **alt rows:** Purl.

3rd row: K22, turn.

5th row: K28, turn.

Cont turning in this manner, working 6 more sts in every knit row until the row "K46(52,58) turn" has been worked.

Next row: As 2nd row.

Cont in st st, inc one st at each end of 7th and foll 6th rows until there are 69(75,81) sts.

Cont until short side measures 16(17,18) cm from beg, ending with a purl row.

Shape crotch

Cast off 3 sts at beg of next 2 rows.

Dec one st at each end of next and foll alt

rows 6 times in all. 51(57,63) sts.

Cont in st st (beg with a purl row) without shaping until work measures 30(34,41) cm from beg, ending with a purl row.

Change to 3 mm needles.

Work 1 row rib as for waistband, dec 6(6,8) sts evenly across. 45(51,55) sts.

Cont in rib for 3 cm, beg and ending with a 2nd row.

Cast off loosely in rib.

LEFT LEG

Work to correspond with Right Leg to ***, noting that buttonhole row will read thus:-Rib to last 22 sts, K2tog, yfwd, rib 20.

1st and alt rows: Knit.

2nd row: P16, turn.

4th row: P22, turn.

Cont turning in this manner, working 6 more sts in every purl row until the row "P46(52,58), turn" has been worked.

Complete to correspond with Left Front reversing shapings.

FRONT BIB

Using back stitch, join front, back and leg seams.

Tie a coloured thread 8 cm either side of centre front seam.

Using 3.75 mm needles and MC, knit up 42 sts evenly between coloured threads.

Next row: K6MC, P30C1, K6MC.

Next row: K6MC, K30C1, K6MC.

Next row: As 1st row.

Next row: K6MC, work 1st row of Graph B across next 30 sts, K6MC.

Next row: K6MC, work 2nd row of Graph B across next 30 sts, K6MC.

Keeping Graph B correct, work 26 more rows.

Next row: Knit.

Rep last row 5 times.

Next row: K6, cast off 30 sts, K6.

RIGHT SHOULDER STRAP

Cont in garter st (every row K) on last 6 sts until strap measures 22(24,25) cm from beg. Cast off.

LEFT SHOULDER STRAP

Join yarn to rem 6 sts and work to correspond with Right Shoulder Strap.

TO MAKE UP

Sew buttons to end of straps. Thread elastic through first, last and centre row of rib at waist. Using knitting stitch and C3, embroider beak. Using C4, embroider eye as illustrated.

BOOTEES

Commence at centre of sole

Using 3.75 mm needles and MC, cast on 35 sts.

1st row: Knit.
2nd row: Purl.
3rd row: K1, inc in next st, K14, inc in next st, K1, inc in next st, K14, inc in next st, K1. 39 sts.
4th row: Purl.
5th row: K1, inc in next st, K16, inc in next st, K1, inc in next st, K16, inc in next st, K1. 43 sts.
6th row: Purl.
7th row: K1, inc in next st, K18, inc in next st, K1, inc in next st, K18, inc in next st, K1. 47 sts.
8th row: Purl.
9th row: K1, inc in next st, K20, inc in next st, K1, inc in next st, K20, inc in next st, K1.

51 sts.
10th row: Knit.
Work 6 rows st st (1 row K, 1 row P), in stripes of 2 rows MC, 2 rows C1 and 2 rows MC.

Shape instep
Using MC
1st row: K30, K2togtbl, turn.
2nd row: P10, P2tog, turn.
3rd row: K10, K2togtbl, turn.
4th row: As 2nd row.
Rep 3rd and 4th rows 6 times.
17th row: Knit to end.
18th row: Purl across all 35 sts.
19th row: K1, *yfwd, K2tog, rep from * to end.
20th row: Purl.
Change to 3 mm needles and C1.

21st row: Knit.
22nd row: K1, *P1, K1, rep from * to end.
Using C2
Rep 21st and 22nd rows once.
Using C1
Rep 21st and 22nd rows once.
Using C1
27th row: K2, *P1, K1, rep from * to last st, K1.
Rep 22nd and 27th rows 3 times.
Cast off loosely in rib.

TO MAKE UP
Press lightly with a damp cloth and a cool iron. Using back stitch, join foot, heel and back seams.
Thread ribbon through eyelet holes and tie in a bow at centre front.

GAUGE YOUR TENSION

Correct tension is essential for perfect fit and shape. This is especially so if changing yarn from one type or brand to another.

What is tension?
Tension, or gauge, is simply a way of measuring the tightness or looseness of your knitting. It is affected by the type and thickness of your yarn, the size of the needles, and whether your knitting will be plain or patterned. Naturally if you are using thicker yarn you will count fewer stitches to the stated length.

If your tension is too loose (too few stitches to the stated length), your garment will lack shape, stretch easily and wash poorly. If your tension is too tight (too many stitches to the stated length), your knitting will feel stiff and will not be as comfortable to wear.

How to measure it?
You must ensure that you have the same number of stitches to the stated length, usually 10 cm, as given in the pattern. To measure tension, knit a tension square in your stitch pattern and count the stitches. It is best to knit a piece bigger than 10 cm square. Cast off then press your sample lightly, if necessary. Pin out your square on a firm surface. Align the top of a ruler with a row of stitches. Place a pin at 0, and another at 10 cm. Count the stitches between the pins. To measure row tension, place the ruler vertically.

Adjusting your tension
If you have fewer stitches to 10 cm, use thinner needles. If you have more stitches to 10 cm, use thicker needles. Remember if you change yarn, needles or pattern, you must knit a new tension square.

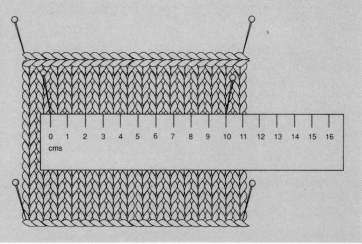

YELLOW SPOTTED DRESS

SIZE: 6 to 12 months

MATERIALS
☐ 1.3 m of 115 cm wide voile
☐ three 1 cm buttons
☐ bias binding
☐ 3 mm wide elastic

PATTERN
Pattern outline ~~~~~~~~~~~~~~~
13 front yoke (cut 2); 14 front skirt (cut 1);15 back yoke (cut 2); 16 back skirt (cut 2); 17 sleeves (cut 2); 18 front/back pants. Cut out pattern pieces as directed. 1 cm seams allowed. Join all pieces together with right sides facing. Cut a piece 80 cm x 8 cm for yoke frill and one 106 cm x 8 cm for skirt frill.

1 Sew front yoke to back yokes at shoulders. Fold bias binding over double. Tack around yoke edge with raw edges even.
2 Fold yoke frill over double with right sides facing. Sew ends. Turn and press. Tack raw edges together and gather. Tack frill around right side of yoke with raw edges even, adjusting gathers to fit.
3 Stitch centre back skirt seam up to opening. Finish skirt back opening edges as desired.
4 Gather upper edge of front and back skirts as far as extension fold. Pin yoke to skirts as far as foldline on back yokes, adjusting gathering to fit. Fold back extensions to inside along foldlines, forming facings. Stitch through all thicknesses, taking care to leave back yoke facing free.
5 Sew shoulder seams of yoke facings. Turn under raw lower edges of facings. Handsew into place. Tack neck edges and armhole edges together.
6 Gather sleeve heads. Sew sleeves into armholes. Press seams and frills towards sleeves and skirt. On outside, topstitch around edge of yoke.
7 Make neck frill as yoke frill. Pin around neck edge with raw edges even. Bind neck with bias binding, fixing frill into place as you go.

8 Turn in 4 cm at sleeve ends. Stitch raw edge down with two rows to form casing and frill. Thread elastic through casing and secure ends.
9 Sew side seams from wrist to hem.
10 Fold bias binding over double and tack around hem with raw edges even. Fold hem frill over double with right sides together. Sew ends together. Turn and press. Gather frill and pin around hem, over bias binding, with raw edges even. Stitch through all thicknesses. Press seam towards skirt. Topstitch around skirt hem, catching seam allowance to skirt.
11 Make buttonholes in back yoke. Sew on buttons.
12 To make pants, sew inside leg seams. Press seams open. Sew crotch seams. Finish raw edges at leg ends with a narrow hem. On the inside zigzag 3 mm wide elastic around legs, stretching elastic slightly as you sew to form a frill. Turn raw edge at waist to inside along foldline. Stitch down, forming casing. Thread elastic through casing and secure ends.

SHEET WITH SPOTS

MATERIALS
- ☐ 150 cm of 115 cm wide cream voile
- ☐ 18 cm of 115 cm wide spotted voile
- ☐ 115 cm yellow bias binding

1 Sew spotted trim to top edge of sheet with right side of trim facing wrong side of sheet. Fold trim over double, with wrong sides together, onto right side of sheet. Press under raw edge.

2 Fold bias binding over double. Pin binding under pressed edge of trim. Stitch along pressed edge, through all thicknesses, fixing bias binding as you go.

3 Turn in 6 mm on all raw edges of sheet. Turn another 1 cm and stitch down. Press.

BABY'S BEDTIME

Keeping your baby comfortably warm and covered all through the night is a breeze with a pretty and practical sleep suit. Blankets and sheets are often kicked off, especially as your baby grows more active. Use a fitted sheet for covering the mattress and a one piece suit, made of a fabric appropriate to the season, which covers little feet. You can choose pure cotton or stretch towelling for those in-between nights and brushed cotton or fine wool in cooler weather. For those really chilly nights, add a zippered or buttoned sleeping bag for extra warmth.

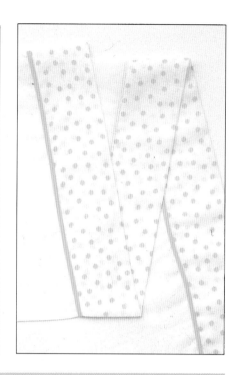

YELLOW STRIPED SLEEP SUIT

SIZE: 0 to 6 months

MATERIALS
- ☐ 1 m of 115 cm wide fabric
- ☐ 45 cm zipper
- ☐ narrow elastic

PATTERN
Pattern outline ━━━━━

7 right front suit (cut 1); 8 left front extension (cut 1); 9 left front suit (cut 1); 10 back suit (cut 2); 11 collar (cut 2); 12 sleeves (cut 2).
Cut out pattern pieces as directed. 1 cm seams allowed. Join all pieces together with right sides facing.

1 Sew right front to left front extension up to A, matching raw edges. Stitch left front to left front extension as far as B.

2 Press in seam allowances on front opening. Sew zipper into place beneath pressed edges with pull tab 1.5 cm below neck seam.

3 Make pleats on outside of both back foot sections as marked. Stitch centre back seam.

4 Cut 70 cm of 2 cm wide self bias. Press bias strip over double, wrong sides facing. Tack length of bias strip to right side of all raglan armhole edges. Pin sleeves to armholes. Stitch through all thicknesses, catching bias as you sew.

5 Tack folded self bias around outside edge of right side of one collar section, keeping raw edges even. Place two collar sections together with right sides facing. Stitch around outside edge. Turn and press.

6 Tack collar around neck edge, clipping neck edge if necessary, and keeping raw edges even. Pin bias strip around neck edge over collar seam, with right sides facing and raw edges even. Stitch. Turn bias to inside. Turn under all raw edges and stitch down.

7 Stitch bias around sleeve ends with raw edges even. Turn raw edges to inside and stitch down, forming casing. Thread narrow elastic through casing. Secure ends of elastic.

8 Sew front to back, stitching in one continuous seam from sleeve end around legs to sleeve end.

9 Make a length of rouleau from bias strip. Tie into bow and stitch very securely by hand to neckline.

First Smiles

A baby's first smile is a special moment to be treasured. Special too, are these lovely garments in traditional pink, blue and white. There's an outfit for every babe, no matter what the time of year, and some sweet touches for the traditional nursery, featuring a bunny or two.

PINK, BLUE AND WHITE BABY'S SHAWL COLLAR CARDIGAN

BACK
Using 2.25 mm needles and MC, cast on 74(82,90) sts.
1st row: K2, * P2, K2, rep from * to end.
2nd row: P2, * K2, P2, rep from * to end.
Rep 1st and 2nd rows until band measures 4 cm from beg, ending with a 2nd row and inc 0(2,2) sts evenly across last row. 74(84,92) sts.
Change to 3 mm needles.
Cont in st st (1 row K, 1 row P) until work measures 14.5(16,18) cm from beg, ending with a purl row.
Shape armholes
Cast off 4(5,5) sts at beg of next 2 rows.
Dec one st at each end of next and foll alt rows 3(4,5) times in all. 60(66,72) sts.
Next row: K2(0,5) inc in next st, * K4(4,3), inc in next st, rep from * to last 2(0,6) sts, K2(0,6). 72(80,88) sts.
Beg Blackberry Stitch patt:
1st row: Knit
2nd row: Using C1, K2, *(K1, P1, K1) in next st, P3tog, rep from * to last 2 sts, K2.
3rd row: Purl
4th row: Using C2, K2, * P3tog, (K1, P1, K1) in next st, rep from * to last 2 sts, K2.
5th row: Purl.
6th row: Using MC, as 2nd row.
7th row: Purl.
8th row: Using C1, as 4th row.
9th row: Purl.
10th row: Using C2, as 2nd row.
11th row: Purl.
12th row: Using MC, as 4th row.
13th row: Purl.
Rows 2 to 13 inclusive form patt.
Work 17(17,19) rows patt.
Cast off loosely.
LEFT FRONT
Using 2.25 mm needles and MC, cast on 34(42,46) sts.
Work 4 cm in rib as for lower band of Back, ending with a 2nd row and inc 3(0,0) sts evenly across last row. 37(42,46) sts.
Change to 3 mm needles.
Cont in st st until work measures 14.5(16,18) cm from beg, ending with a

MEASUREMENTS

To fit underarm cm	41	46	51
ins	16	18	20
Actual measurement			
cm	45	51	56
Length to back neck			
cm	23	25	28
Sleeve seam cm	13	15.5	18.5

MATERIALS
Cleckheaton Babysoft 3 ply (25 g) balls (or other suitable 3 ply): 5(5,6) balls of Main Colour (MC), 1 ball each of 1st and 2nd Contrasts (C1 — Blue), (C2 — Pink); 1 pair each 3 mm (No. 11) and 2.25 mm (No. 13) knitting needles or the required size to give correct tension; 6 Buttons.

TENSION
This garment has been designed at a tension of 32 sts to 10 cm over st st, using 3 mm needles and 40 sts to 10 cm over Blackberry Stitch, using 3 mm needles.
It is important to knit a tension square and to work to the stated tension in order to obtain the required measurements. If your square is bigger use finer needles. If your square is smaller use thicker needles.

purl row. **
Shape armhole and front slope
Next row: Cast off 4(5,5) sts, knit to last 2 sts, K2tog.
Dec one st at armhole edge in alt rows 3(4,5) times, AT SAME TIME dec one st at

neck edge in alt rows 3(4,5) times, 26(28,30) sts.
Purl one row, inc 6(7,8) sts evenly across. 32(35,38) sts.
Beg Blackberry Stitch patt
1st row: Knit to last 2 sts, K2tog.
2nd row: Using C1, K1(0,3), * (K1, P1, K1) in next st, P3tog, rep from * to last 2 sts, K2.
3rd row: Purl to last 2 sts, P2tog.
4th row: Using C2, K0(3,2), * P3tog, (K1, P1, K1) in next st, rep from * to last 2 sts, K2.
5th row: As 3rd row.
6th row: Using MC, K3(2,1), * (K1, P1, K1) in next st, P3tog, rep from * to last 2 sts, K2.
Keeping Blackberry Stitch correct as placed in last 5 rows, dec one st at neck edge in next row and foll alt row/s 2(2,1) time/s, then in foll 4th rows 4(4,5) times. 22(25,28) sts.
Work 3 rows.
Cast off loosely.
RIGHT FRONT
Work as for Left Front to **
Shape armhole and front slope
Next row: K2tog, knit to end.
Next row: Cast off 4(5,5) sts, purl to end.
Dec one st at armhole edge in next and foll alt rows 3(4,5) times in all, AT SAME TIME dec one st at neck edge in next and foll alt rows 3(4,5) times in all. 26(28,30) sts.
Purl one row, inc 6(7,8) sts evenly across. 32(35,38) sts.
Beg Blackberry Stitch patt
1st row: K2tog, knit to end.
2nd row: Using C1, K2, * (K1, P1, K1) in next st, P3tog, rep from * to last 1(0,3) st/s, K1(0,3).
3rd row: P2tog, purl to end.
4th row: Using C2, K2, * P3tog, (K1, P1, K1) in next st, rep from * to last 0(3,2) sts, K0(3,2).
5th row: As 3rd row.
6th row: Using MC, K2, * (K1, P1, K1) in next st, P3tog, rep from * to last 3(2,1) st/s, K3(2,1).
Keeping Blackberry Stitch correct as placed in last 5 rows, complete to correspond with Left Front.
SLEEVES
Using 2.25 mm needles and MC, cast on 42(42,46) sts.
Work 4 cm rib as for lower band of Back, ending with a 2nd row and inc 6 sts evenly across last row, 48(48,52) sts.
Change to 3 mm needles.

Cont in st st, inc one st at each end of 3rd row and foll 4th(4th,6th) rows until there are 54(58,58) sts, then in foll 6th(6th,8th) rows until there are 60(64,66) sts.

Cont in st st without shaping until side edge measures 13(15.5,18.5) cm from beg, ending with a purl row.

Shape top

Cast off 2(3,3) sts at beg of next 2 rows.

Dec one st at each end of next row and foll alt rows until 44(44,40) sts rem, then in every row until 14 sts rem.

Cast off.

RIGHT FRONT BAND

Using 2.25 mm needles and MC, cast on 11 sts.

1st row: K1, * P1, K1, rep from * to end.

Rep 1st row for patt.

Work 3 rows patt.

5th row: Patt 4, cast off 2 sts, patt 5.

6th row: Patt 5, cast on 2 sts, patt 4.

Work 12(14,14) rows patt.

Rep 5th and 6th rows once, then work 18(18,20) rows patt. Rep last 20(20,22) rows 3 times more, then 5th and 6th rows once.***

Shape collar

Keeping patt correct, inc one st at end of next and foll alt rows 5 times in all, then in foll 4th rows until there are 25 sts.

Work 47(49,53) rows patt.

Cast off loosely.

LEFT FRONT BAND

Work as for Right Front Band to ***, omit-

---

ting buttonholes.

Shape collar

Keeping patt correct, inc one st at beg of next and foll alt rows 5 times in all, then in foll 4th rows until there are 25 sts.

Work 47(49,53) rows.

Cast off loosely.

TO MAKE UP

Press lightly on wrong side with cool iron, except collar. Using back stitch, join shoulder seams, side and sleeve seams, then sew in sleeves. Using a flat seam, sew Front Bands in position, and join seam at centre back gathering extra to fit at back neck. Fold collar section onto right side. Sew on buttons.

BLACKBERRY STITCH BOOTEES

Using MC, cast on 43 sts.

1st row: (K1, inc in next st, K18, inc in next st) twice, K1. 47 sts.

2nd and alt rows: Knit

3rd row: (K1, inc in next st, K20, inc in next st) twice, K1. 51 sts.

5th row: (K1, inc in next st, K22, inc in next st) twice, K1. 55 sts.

7th row: (K1, inc in next st, K24, inc in next st) twice, K1. 59 sts.

9th row: (K1, inc in next st, K26, inc in next st) twice, K1. 63 sts.

11th row: (K1, inc in next st, K28, inc in next st) twice, K1. 67 sts.

12th row: K2tog, K63, K2tog. 65 sts.

Beg Blackberry Stitch patt

1st row: Knit

2nd row: Using C1, K2, *(K1, P1, K1) in next st, P3tog, rep from * to last 3 sts, k3.

3rd row: Purl

4th row: Using C2, K2, *P3tog, (K1,P1,K1) in next st, rep from * to last 3 sts, K3.

5th row: Purl

6th row: Using MC, as 2nd row.

7th row: Purl

8th row: Using CI, as 4th row

9th row: Purl

10th row: Using C2, as 2nd row.

11th row: Purl

12th row: Using MC, as 4th row.

MEASUREMENTS

To fit foot length 8-9 cm approx

NOTE: For slightly smaller bootees, use one size smaller needles than those which give you the correct tension. For slightly larger bootees, use one size larger needles than those which give you the correct tension.

MATERIALS

Cleckheaton Babysoft 3 Ply (25 g) balls (or other suitable 3 ply): 1 ball Main Colour (MC) and 1 ball each of 1st and 2nd Contrasts (C1 — Blue) (C2 — Pink); 1 pair 3 mm (No.11) knitting needles or the required size to give correct tension, length of ribbon.

TENSION

These bootees have been designed at a tension of 32 sts to 10 cm over st st, using 3 mm needles.

It is important to knit a tension square and to work to the stated tension in order to obtain the required measurements. If your square is bigger use finer needles. If your square is smaller use thicker needles.

Shape instep

Next row: K27 MC, using C1, K10, K2tog, turn.

Next row: Using C1, s1 1, K9, K2tog, turn.

Rep last row until 45 sts rem (17 sts on each side of instep).

Next row: Using C1, K10, K2tog, using MC, knit to end.

Next row: Using MC, Purl. 44 sts.

ANKLE

Next row: K1, *yfwd, K2tog, rep from * to last st, K1.

Next row: Purl, inc 1 st in centre. 45 sts.

Next row: K2, *P1, K1, rep from * to last st, K1.

Next row: K1, *P1, K1, rep from * to end.

Rep last two rows 4 times.

Purl 2 rows.

Rep rows 2 to 12 of Blackberry Stitch pattern once.

Work 3 rows garter stitch (every row K).

Cast off

TO MAKE UP

Using a flat seam, join foot and back seam, reversing back seam above rib. Thread ribbon through eyelet holes, and tie a bow as illustrated. Fold ankle section above rib to right side.

BABY'S BLUE AND WHITE JUMPER AND LEGGINGS

JUMPER
BACK
Using 2.75 mm needles and MC, cast on 59(67,73) sts.

1st row: K2, *P1, K1, rep from * to last st, K1.

2nd row: K1, *P1, K1, rep from * to end.
Rep 1st and 2nd rows until band measures 3(3,4) cm from beg, ending with a 2nd row.
Change to 3.25 mm needles and beg patt.

1st and alt rows: Knit.

2nd row: K4(8,1), P1, *K9, P1, rep from * to last 4(8,1) st/s, K4(8,1).

4th row: K3(7,0), P3, *K7, P3, rep from * to last 3(7,0) sts, K3(7,0).

6th row: K2(0,0), P5(1,4), *K5, P5, rep from * to last 2(6,9) sts, K2(5, 5), P0(1,4).

8th row: K1(0, 0), P7(2,5), *K3, P7, rep from * to last 1(5,8) st/s, K1(3,3), P0(2,5).

10th row: P9(3,6), * K1, P9, rep from * to last 0(4,7) sts, K0(1,1), P0(3, 6).

12th row: K9(3,6), * P1, K9, rep from * to last 0(4,7) sts, P0(1,1), K0(3,6).

14th row: P1(0,0), K7(2,5), *P3, K7, rep from * to last 1(5,8) st/s, P1(3, 3), K0(2,5).

16th row: P2(0,0), K5(1,4), * P5, K5, rep from * to last 2(6,9) sts, P2(5,5), K0(1,4).

18th row: P3(0,0), K3(0,3), *P7, K3, rep from * to last 3(7,0) sts, P3(7,0).

20th row: P4(8,1), K1, *P9, K1, rep from * to last 4(8,1) st/s, P4(8,1).
Rows 1 to 20 inclusive form patt.
Cont in patt until work measures 12(14.5,16.5) cm from beg, working last row on wrong side.**

Divide for back opening
1st row: K32(36,39), turn. Cont on these 32(36,39) sts.

2nd row: K5, patt to end.

3rd row: Knit.
Rep 2nd and 3rd rows once, then 2nd row once.

7th row: K28(32,35), cast off 2 sts, K2.

8th row: K2, cast on 2 sts, K1, patt to end.
Keeping patt correct, and garter st (every row K) correct at left edge, work 10(10,12) rows.

MEASUREMENTS
To fit underarm				
cm		41	46	51
ins		16	18	20
Jumper actual measurements				
cm		45	50	55
Length to back neck				
cm		22	25	28
Sleeve seam	cm	13.5	16	19
Leggings outside leg length				
cm		31	34	37

MATERIALS
Cleckheaton Babysoft 4 ply (25 g) balls (or other suitable 4 ply): 4(5,5) Main Colour (MC), 1 ball Contrast (C) for Jumper; 4(5,5) balls MC, 1 ball C for Leggings; 1 pair each 3.25 mm (No. 10) and 2.75 mm (No. 12) knitting needles or the required size to give correct tension; 3 stitch holders; 4 buttons; tapestry needle for embroidery; length of round elastic for Leggings.

TENSION
30 sts to 10 cm over st st, using 3.25 mm needles and 26 sts to 10 cm over patt, using 3.25 mm needles.
It is important to knit a tension square and to work to the stated tension in order to obtain the required measurements. If your square is bigger use finer needles. If your square is smaller use thicker needles.

Rep last 12(12,14) rows once, then first 6(8,8) of these 12(12,14) rows once. 3 buttonholes.

Shape shoulder
Keeping patt correct, cast off 6(7,8) sts at beg of next row and foll alt row, then 7(8,9) sts at beg of foll alt row. ***
Work 1 row.
Leave rem 13(14,14) sts on a stitch holder.
Join yarn to rem sts at centre, cast on 5 sts for underlap, and knit to end.

2nd row: Patt to last 5 sts, K5.

3rd row: Knit.
Rep 2nd and 3rd rows 17(18,20) times.
Shape shoulder
Complete as for other shoulder to ***.
Leave rem l3(14,14) sts on a stitch holder.

FRONT
Work as for Back to **.
Work 22(24,26) rows patt.

Shape neck
Next row: K24(27,30), turn.
**** Keeping patt correct, dec one st at neck edge in alt rows 5 times.
Work 3(3,5) rows.****

Shape shoulder
Cast off 6(7,8) sts at beg of next row and foll alt row.
Work 1 row. Cast off.
Slip next 11(13,13) sts onto a stitch holder and leave.
Join yarn to rem sts and knit to end.
Rep from **** to ****.
Work 1 row.

Shape shoulder
Complete as for other shoulder.

SLEEVES
Using 2.75 mm needles and MC, cast on 35(37,39) sts.
Work 3(3,4) cm in rib as for lower band of Back, ending with a 2nd row, and inc 12(12,14) sts evenly across last row. 47(49,53) sts.
Change to 3.25 mm needles and beg patt.
Cont in patt noting to foll 2nd size of Back for **1st Size of Sleeves**, 1st size of Back for **2nd Size of Sleeves**, and 3rd size of Back for **3rd Size of Sleeves**, until work measures 13.5(16,l9) cm from beg, working last row on wrong side.

Shape top
Keeping patt correct, cast off 6(6,7) sts at beg of next 6 rows.
Cast off.

NECKBAND
Using back stitch, join shoulder seams. With right side facing, using 2.75 mm needles and MC, knit up 63(67,71) sts

evenly around neck edge, including sts from stitch holders. Work 5 rows rib as for lower band of Back, beg with a 2nd row.
6th row: Rib to last 4 sts, cast off 2 sts, rib 2.
7th row: Rib 2, cast on 2 sts, rib to end. Work 2 rows rib.
Cast off loosely in rib.

TO MAKE UP
Tie coloured threads 9.5(10,11) cm down from each shoulder seam. Using back stitch, sew in sleeves evenly between coloured threads. Join side and sleeve seams. Sew underlap in position. Sew on buttons. Using knitting stitch and C, embroider triangles on Front, beg at centre approx 11 cm down from neck shaping and extending diagonally outwards as illustrated (see Graph A).

LEGGINGS
RIGHT LEG (Beg at waist)
Using 2.75 mm needles and MC, cast on 81(85,89) sts.
1st row: K2, *P1, K1, rep from * to last st, K1.
2nd row: K1, *P1, K1, rep from * to end.
Rep 1st and 2nd rows twice, inc 1 st in centre of last row. 82(86,90) sts.
Change to 3.25 mm needles.
Work 2 rows st st.
Shape back
NOTE: To avoid holes when turning, bring yarn to front of work, slip next st onto right hand needle, ybk sl st back onto left hand needle, then turn and proceed as instructed. ****
1st row: K14(16,18) turn.
2nd and alt rows: Purl.

3rd row: K21(23,25), turn.
5th row: K28(30,32), turn.
7th row: K35(37,39), turn.
9th row: K42(44,46), turn.
Cont turning in this manner, working 7 more sts in alt rows until the row "K70(72,74), turn" has been worked.
Next row: Purl.
*****Cont in st st, inc 1 st at each end of 11th and foll 10th(12th,14th) rows until there are 88(92, 96) sts. Cont until shorter edge measures 16(17,19) cm from beg, ending with a purl row. Tie a coloured thread at end of last row to denote back edge.
Shape leg
Dec 1 st at each end of next and foll 3rd rows until 58(66,86) sts rem, then in foll 4th rows until 56(60,64) sts rem. Cont in st st until side edge measures 15.5(17.5,19.5) cm from coloured thread, ending with a purl row and dec 15 sts evenly across last row. 41(45,49) sts.
Change to 2.75 mm needles and work 12 rows rib as for waist dec 1 st at end of last row. 40(44, 48) sts. Change to 3.25 mm needles. *****
Divide for foot
1st row: K37(40,43), turn.
2nd row: P14, turn. Work 14(16,18) rows on these 14 sts. Break off yarn and slip these sts onto a stitch holder.
With right side facing, rejoin yarn to inside edge where sts were left, knit up 12(13,14) sts along side of instep, knit across 14 sts on needle (inc 1 st in centre), knit up 12(13,14) sts along other side of instep, then knit across rem 3(4,5) sts. 65(71,77) sts.

GRAPH A

☐ K st on odd rows, P st on even rows (MC)

☑ K st on even rows (MC)

☒ C (embroidered on afterwards)

GRAPH B

☒ C (embroidered on afterwards)

Knit 13 rows garter stitch.
Shape foot
1st row: K7(8,9), (K2tog, K2) twice, K25(28,31), (K2tog, K1) twice, K19(21,23). 61(67,73) sts.
2nd and alt rows: Knit.
3rd row: K6(7,8), (K2tog, K2) twice, K23(26,29), (K2tog, K1) twice, K18(20,22). 57(63,69) sts.
5th row: K5(6,7), (K2tog, K2) twice, K21(24, 27), (K2tog, K1) twice, K17(19, 21). 53(59, 65) sts.
7th row: K4(5,6), (K2tog, K2) twice, K19(22,25), (K2tog, K1) twice, K16(18, 20). 49(55,61) sts.
Cast off.

LEFT LEG (Beg at waist)
Work as for Right Leg to ****.
1st and alt rows: Knit.
2nd row: P14(16,18), turn.
4th row: P21(23,25), turn.
6th row: P28(30,32), turn.
8th row: P35(37,39), turn.
10th row: P42(44,46), turn.
Cont turning in this manner, working 7 sts more in alt rows until the row "P70(72,74) turn" has been worked.
Work as for Right Leg from ***** to *****, noting to tie the coloured thread at beg of the relevant row, instead of at the end.
Divide for foot
1st row: K17(18,19), turn.
2nd row: P14, turn.
Work 14(16,18) rows on these 14 sts. Break off yarn and slip these sts onto a stitch holder.
With right side facing, rejoin yarn to inside edge where sts were left, knit up 12(13,14) sts along side of instep, knit across 14 sts on needle (inc one st in centre), knit up 12(13, 14) sts along other side of instep, then knit across rem 26(29, 34) sts. 65(71,77) sts.
Knit 13 rows garter stitch.
Shape foot
1st row: K20(22,24), (K2tog, K1) twice, K26(29,32), (K2tog, K2) twice, K5(6,7). 61(67,73) sts.

2nd and alt rows: Knit.
3rd row: K19(21,23), (K2tog, K1) twice, K24(27,30), (K2tog, K2) twice, K4(5,6). 57(63,69) sts.
5th row: K18(20, 22),(K2tog, K1) twice, K22(25,28), (K2tog, K2) twice, K3(4,5). 53(59,65) sts.
7th row: K17(19, 21), (K2tog, K1) twice, K20(23,26), (K2tog, K2) twice, K2(3,4). 49(55,61) sts. Cast off.

TO MAKE UP

Using knitting stitch and C, embroider one triangle in centre of each instep as for Graph B. Using back stitch, join back, front, leg and foot seams. Thread round elastic through 1st, 3rd, and 5th rows of rib at waist.

PINK AND WHITE BABY'S CARDIGAN

BACK

Using 2.75 mm needles and MC, cast on 71(77,83,89) sts.
1st row: K2, * P1, K1, rep from * to last st, K1.
2nd row: K1, * P1, K1, rep from * to end.
Rep 1st and 2nd rows until band measures 3 cm from beg, ending with a 2nd row and inc one st at end of last row. 72(78,84,90) sts.
Change to 3.25 mm needles.
Using C
Work 2 rows st st (1 row K, 1 row P).
Beg patt
NOTE: Always slip sts purlways in patt.
1st row: Using MC, K2, sl2, * K4, sl2, rep from * to last 2 sts, K2.
2nd row: K1, P1, sl2, P1, * K2, P1, sl2, P1, rep from * to last st, K1.
3rd row: Using C, K1, "C2F", "C2B", * K2, "C2F", "C2B", rep from * to last st, K1.
4th row: Purl.
Rows 1 to 4 inclusive form patt.
Cont in patt until work measures 13(15,18,21) cm from beg, working last row on wrong side.
Shape armholes
Keeping patt correct, cast off 5 sts at beg of next 2 rows.
Dec one st at each end of next and alt rows

MEASUREMENTS

To fit underarm

	cm	41	46	51	56
	ins	16	18	20	22
Actual measurement					
	cm	46	51	56	61
Length to back neck					
	cm	23	26	30	34
Sleeve seam					
	cm	14	17	20	24

MATERIALS

Cleckheaton Babysoft 4 ply (25 g) balls (or other suitable 4 ply): 4(4,5,5) balls Main Colour (MC — Pink), 3(3,4,4) balls Contrast (C — White) ; 1 pair each 3.25 mm (No. 10) and 2.27 mm (No. 12) knitting needles or the required size to give correct tension; 4(4,5,5) buttons.

ABBREVIATIONS

"C2F" = Knit in to front of 2nd st on left hand needle, then into front of first st, slipping both sts of needle tog.
"C2B" = Knit into back of 2nd st on left hand needle, then in back of first st, slipping both sts off needle tog.

TENSION

2 patts to 4 cm in width, using 3.25 mm needles and 30 sts to 10 cm over st st, using 3.25 mm needles.
It is important to knit a tension square and to work to the stated tension in order to obtain the required measurements. If your square is bigger use finer needles. If your square is smaller use thicker needles.

until 52(58,64,70) sts rem.
Work 37(41,47,51) rows.
Shape shoulders
Keeping patt correct, cast off 7(8,9,11) sts at beg of next 2 rows, then 7(9,10,11) sts at beg of foll 2 rows.
Cast off rem 24(24,26,26) sts.
LEFT FRONT
Using 2.75 mm needles and MC, cast on 35(37,41,43) sts.
Work in rib as given for lower band of Back, until band measures 3 cm from beg, ending with a 2nd row and inc one st at end of last row. 36(38,42,44) sts.
Change to 3.25 mm needles.
Using C
Work 2 rows st st.
Beg patt **.
1st row: Using MC, K2, sl2, *K4, sl2, rep from * to last 2(4,2,4) sts, K2(4,2,4).
2nd row: P0(1,0,1), K1(2,1,2), P1, sl2, P1, *K2, P1, sl2, P1, rep from * to last st, K1.
3rd row: Using C, K1, "C2F", "C2B", *K2, "C2F", "C2B", rep from * to last 1(3,1,3) st/s, K1(3,1,3).
4th row: Purl.
Rows 1 to 4 inclusive form patt.
Cont in patt until work measures same as Back to underarm, ending with same row.
Shape armhole and front slope
Keeping patt correct, cast off 5 sts at beg of next row.
Dec 1 st at armhole edge in alt rows 5 times, AT SAME TIME dec 1 st at front edge in 2nd and foll alt(4th,4th,4th) rows 3(9,12,7) times in all, then in foll 4th(6th, 6th, 6th) row/s until 14(17,19,22) sts rem.

Work 5 rows.

Shape shoulder

Cast off 7(8,9,11) sts at beg of next row.

Work 1 row.

Cast off.

RIGHT FRONT

Work as given for Left Front to **.

1st row: Using MC, K2(4,2,4), * sl2, K4, rep from * to last 4 sts, sl2, K2.

2nd row: K1, P1, sl2, P1, * K2, P1, sl2, P1, rep from * to last 1(3,1,3) st/s, K1(2,1,2), P0(1,0,1).

3rd row: Using C, K1(3,1,3), * "C2F", "C2B", K2, rep from * to last 5 sts, "C2F", "C2B", K1.

4th row: Purl.

Rows 1 to 4 inclusive form patt.

Cont in patt, until work measures same as Back to underarm, working last row on right side.

Shape armhole and front slope

Keeping patt correct, cast off 5 sts at beg of next row.

Dec one st at armhole edge in next and alt rows 5 times in all, AT SAME TIME dec one st at front edge in next and foll

alt(4th,4th,4th) rows 3(9,12,7) times in all, then in foll 4th(6th,6th,6th) row/s until 14(17,19,22) sts rem.

Work 6 rows.

Shape shoulder

Complete as for other shoulder.

SLEEVES

Using 2.75 mm needles and MC, cast on 37(37,39,41) sts.

Work in rib as given for lower band of Back until band measures 3 cm from beg, ending with a 2nd row and inc 5(5,9,7) sts evenly across last row. 42(42,48,48) sts. Change to 3.25 mm needles.

Work in patt as given for Back, inc one st at each end of 5th and foll 6th(8th,10th,12th) row/s until there are 54(56,52,62) sts, **3rd size only** – then in foll 12th rows until there are 60 sts, working extra sts into patt.

Cont in patt without shaping until side edge measures 14(17,20,24) cm from beg, working last row on wrong side.

Shape top

Keeping patt correct, cast off 3 sts at beg of next 2 rows.

Dec 1 st at each end of next row.

Work 1(3,3,3) row/s.

Dec 1 st at each end of next and foll alt rows until 14 sts rem.

Work 1 row. Cast off.

FRONT BAND

Using back stitch, join shoulder seams.

Using 2.75 mm needles, cast on 11 sts.

1st row: K2, (P1, K1), 4 times, K1.

2nd row: K1, (P1, K1), 5 times

Rep 1st and 2nd rows once.

5th row: Rib 5, cast off 2 sts, rib 4.

6th row: Rib 4, cast on 2 sts, rib 5.

Work 18(20,18,22) rows rib.

Rep last 20(22,20,24) rows 2(2,3,3) times, then 5th and 6th rows once. 4(4,5,5) buttonholes.

Cont in rib without buttonholes until band is length required to fit (slightly stretched) along fronts and across back of neck.

Cast off loosely in rib.

TO MAKE UP

Using back stitch, join side and sleeve seams. Sew in Sleeves. Sew Front Band in position. Sew on buttons.

WHITE PANTS WITH CONTRAST CUFFS

SIZE: 6 to 12 months

MATERIALS

☐ 50 cm of 115 cm wide white cotton

☐ remnant of printed cotton for piping and cuffs

☐ 1 cm wide elastic to fit

PATTERN

Pattern outline ━ ━ ━ ━ ━

20 front pants (cut 2); 20 back pants (cut 2); 20a leg facings (cut 4)

Using overall pattern, cut out pattern pieces as directed, omitting bib and straps.

NOTE: These pants, unlike the overalls, have side seams, so cut along marked side seam line, remembering to add 1 cm seam allowance on both sides of side seam on fronts and backs. 1 cm seam allowed on all other seams. Join all pieces

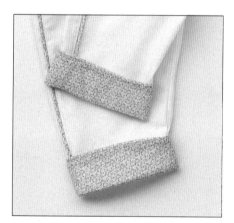

together with right sides facing. Trace leg facings off legs as separate pieces.

1 Make sufficient piping to trim both side seams and cuff edges. Tack piping to right side of fronts with raw edges even.

2 Sew inside leg seams. Sew crotch seams. Sew side seams with piping in between.

3 Tack piping around right side of leg ends with raw edges even. Sew side seams of facings. Place facings around leg ends, with right sides facing and raw edges

even. Stitch through all thicknesses. Turn facings to inside. Turn in raw edges and stitch down. Turn cuffs to right side.

4 Neaten raw edge at waist by overlock, zigzag or straight stitching. Turn neatened raw edge at waist to inside. Press. Stitch finished edge down, forming casing, leaving small opening for inserting elastic. Thread elastic through casing, adjust length and secure ends.

SUNSUIT WITH BUNNY APPLIQUE

SIZE: 0 to 6 months

MATERIALS
- ☐ 70 cm of 115 cm wide cotton
- ☐ scrap of pink fabric for applique
- ☐ 11 hammer-on snaps
- ☐ 75 cm of 1 cm wide elastic
- ☐ small amount fusible interfacing

PATTERN
Pattern outline • • • • • • • • • • • • • • • • •
5 upper front (cut 4, two are for facing); 6 back and lower front (cut 2, one is for lining)
Cut out pattern pieces as directed. Trace, cut out and interface applique motif. 1 cm seams allowed. Join all pieces together with right sides facing.

1 Sew motif onto left front, using narrow zigzag stitches. Trim fabric close to stitching. Stitch again using wider satin stitch, covering raw edge and previous stitching.
2 Stitch shoulder seams of suit and of lining. Pin suit and lining together with right sides facing. Stitch, leaving waist edge of front open. Reinforce corners with double stitching. Trim seams, cut into corners and clip curves. Turn and press.
3 To form leg casings, run two rows of stitching around curved leg ends from A to B. Cut two 29 cm lengths of elastic and insert into casings through open waist edge. Secure ends.
4 To form waist casing, neaten raw edges together, by overlock, zigzag or straight stitching, and turn in 1.5 cm. Press casing to inside along foldline. Stitch. Thread 17 cm elastic through casing. Smooth out elastic at each end of casing and stitch through casing about 1.5 cm from each end. Pull out ends of elastic and trim off excess. Stitch once more across ends of casing.
5 Overlap fronts with centres matching. Hammer on studs, according to manufacturer's instructions, as shown on pattern. Attach front to back at sides with one hammer-on stud at large dot.

BABY BLUE SUNHAT

SIZE: 0 to 6 months

MATERIALS
- ☐ 20 cm of 115 cm wide poplin
- ☐ fusible interfacing

PATTERN
Pattern outline ━ • • • ━ • • • grey
21 crown (cut 6); 22 brim (cut 4)
Cut out pattern pieces as directed. 1 cm seams allowed. Join all pieces together with right sides facing.

1 Interface brim sections. Sew centre front and centre back seams of brim and of brim facing. Sew facing to brim around outside edge with right sides together. Tack raw edges together. Beginning right at edge of brim, stitch around brim in a snail pattern right up to crown edge, using a continuous stitching line.
2 Sew three crown sections together to form half crown. Sew two halves together.
3 Sew crown to brim. Neaten raw edge and turn seam towards crown. Stitch seam allowance to crown. Make small bow or fabric-covered button and fix to top.

BUNNY CUSHION

The secret of this cushion lies in the choice of fabric with a clear motif on a squared background. Stitching around motifs and squares, using an embroidery hoop, gives the impression of quilting. You will see that we have appliqued the motif onto a sun-suit and embroidered it onto a sheet.

MATERIALS
- [ ] 35 cm of 115 cm wide cotton print fabric for cushion front and back; 2 m of 10 cm wide strip of complementary cotton print for ruffle
- [ ] 3 m cotton lace
- [ ] 30 cm cushion insert
- [ ] 25 cm zipper
- [ ] 1.40 m piping
- [ ] 35 cm x 35 cm thin wadding (batting)
- [ ] short quilters' needles
- [ ] embroidery hoop
- [ ] quilters' sewing thread or similar

PATTERN
Cut one square 32 cm x 32 cm for cushion front and two pieces 17 cm x 32 cm for back, taking care to centre pattern squares and motifs. You may need to alter these measurements to suit your chosen fabric.

1 Tack cushion front to a piece of thin wadding. Using an embroidery hoop, double thread and short needle handsew around motifs and squares with a small running stitch, through all thicknesses.
2 Tack piping around edge of right side of cushion front with raw edges even. Join ends of ruffle. Press under one raw edge of ruffle. Sew lace beneath this edge. Gather other edge of ruffle. Sew ruffle around right side of cushion front with raw edges even. Stitch through all thicknesses, fixing piping as you go.

3 Sew centre seam of cushion back, leaving opening for zipper. Sew zipper between pressed edges.
4 Place cushion front and back together with right sides facing. Stitch around all edges. Turn and press.

EMBROIDERED BUNNY SHEET

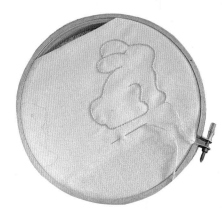

MATERIALS
- [ ] 1.5 m of 115 cm wide fine white cotton
- [ ] embroidery thread

1 Fold in 10 cm at top edge of sheet. Tack along raw edge and again along fold. Trace off design for embroidery from applique motif onto top of right side of sheet, placing tips of ears 1.5 cm from folded edge and about 10 cm apart.
2 Embroider bunnies in chain stitch with two threads of embroidery floss. An embroidery hoop makes this easier to manage *(see below)*.
3 Fold embroidered section again. Press. Stitch along edge.
3 Turn in 6 mm along raw edges of sheet. Turn another 1 cm and stitch hem into place. Press.

Keep those bugs away from your precious baby. Trim a large square of net with wide lace and ribbons for a really pretty mosquito net.

> ## ♡ HINT ♡
>
> *An embroidery hoop will ensure perfectly even embroidery as it holds the fabric firm and smooth.*

Sleepy Time

Your baby will always have sweet dreams tucked into this lovely set of matching sheets, cot bumper and "snug as a bug" knitted cover. The secret is all in the pleasing combination of colours and patterns. Add a sleepsuit, trimmed to match, and a delightfully cosy, knitted sleeping bag for those extra chilly nights.

FAIR ISLE COT COVER

NOTE: When working in Fair Isle patt, DO NOT WEAVE COLOURS but carry colour not in use loosely across on wrong side of work. Always carry colours to end of row.

Using 4 mm needles and MC, cast on 161 sts.

1st row: K4MC, *K3C1, K3MC, rep from * to last st, K1MC.

2nd row: P4MC, * P3C1, P3MC, rep from * to last st, K1MC.

Rep 1st and 2nd rows once.

Rep 1st and 2nd rows twice, using C1 in place of MC, and MC in place of C1.

Rep last 8 rows once.

17th row: K4MC, K3C1, K3MC, K3C1, K3C2, * K3MC, K3C2, rep from * to last 13 sts, K3C1, K3MC, K3C1, K4MC.

18th row: P4MC, P3C1, P3MC, P3C1, P3C2, * P3MC, P3C2, rep from * to last 13 sts, P3C1, P3MC, P3C1, P4MC.

Rep last 2 rows once.

21st row: K4C1, K3MC, K3C1, K3MC, K3C2, *K3MC, K3C2, rep from * to last 13 sts, K3MC, K3C1, K3MC, K4C1.

22nd row: P4C1, P3MC, P3C1, P3MC, P3C2, * P3MC, P3C2, rep from * to last 13 sts, P3MC, P3C1, P3MC, P4C1.

Rep last 2 rows once.

25th row: K4MC, K3C1, K3MC, K3C1, * K8C3, K1MC, rep from * to last 13 sts, K3C1, K3MC, K3C1, K4MC.

26th row: P4MC, P3C1, P3MC, P3C1, * P2MC, P7C3, rep from * to last 13 sts, P3C1, P3MC, P3C1, P4MC.

27th row: K4MC, K3C1, K3MC, K3C1, * K6C3, K3MC, rep from * to last 13 sts, K3C1, K3MC, K3C1, K4MC.

28th row: P4MC, P3C1, P3MC, P3C1, *P4MC, P5C3, rep from * to last 13 sts, P3C1, P3MC, P3C1, P4MC.

29th row: K4C1, K3MC, K3C1, K3MC, *K4C3, K5C3, rep from * to last 13 sts, K3MC, K3C1, K3MC, K4C1.

30th row: P4C1, P3MC, P3C1, P3MC, *P6MC, P3C3, rep from * to last 13 sts, P3MC, P3C1, P3MC, P4C1.

31st row: K4C1, K3MC, K3C1, K3MC, *K2C3, K7MC, rep from * to last 13 sts, K3MC, K3C1, K3MC, K4C1.

32nd row: P4C1, P3MC, P3C1, P3MC, *P8MC, P1C3, rep from * to last 13 sts, P3MC, P3C1, P3MC, P4C1.

Rep first 8 rows twice.

Rep rows 25 to 32 inclusive once, noting to keep colours correct in border patt, but to use C4 in place of MC, and MC in place of C3 for triangle patt.

Rep rows 17 to 24 inclusive once.

Last 64 rows form patt.

Cont in patt until work measures approx 100 cm from beg, ending with an 8th or 40th patt row.

Using MC, cont in st st (1 row K, 1 row P) until MC section measures same as patt section, ending with a purl row.

Cast off loosely.

TO MAKE UP

Fold knitting in half (foldline is at end of patt section), so that right sides are together. Join 2 sides and turn inside out. Place wadding inside and close rem side, using small stitches. Using 2 strands of C1 and small even running stitches, sew around inside of border, noting to sew through 3 thicknesses (including wadding).

MEASUREMENTS
Size: 64 x 100 cm

MATERIALS
Cleckheaton 5 ply Machine Wash (50 g) balls (or other suitable 5 ply): 9 balls Main Colour (MC — White), 3 balls 1st Contrast (C1 — Blue), 1 ball each of 2nd, 3rd and 4th Contrasts (C2 — Apricot) (C3 — Lilac), (C4 — Coral), 1 pair each 4 mm (No. 8) and 3.75 mm (No. 9) knitting needles or the required size to give correct tension; length of wadding (approx 62 cm x 100 cm).

TENSION
This Cot Cover has been designed at a tension of 26 sts to 10 cm over st st, using 3.75 mm needles, and 26 sts to 10 cm over Fair Isle patt, using 4 mm needles.

It is important to knit a tension square and to work to the stated tension in order to obtain the required measurements. If your square is bigger use finer needles. If your square is smaller use thicker needles.

Fair Isle Cot Cover

BABY'S SLEEPING BAG

BACK
Using 3.25 mm needles and C2, cast on 81(85,93) sts.

1st row: K2, * P1, K1, rep from * to last st, K1.

2nd row: K1, * P1, K1, rep from * to end.
Rep 1st and 2nd rows once.

5th row: Rib 5(7,6), * yfwd, work 2tog, rib 12(12,14), rep from * to last 6(8,7) sts, yfwd, work 2tog, rib 4(6,5). 6 buttonholes.

6th row: As 2nd row.

Rep 1st and 2nd rows until band measures 10 cm from beg, ending with a 2nd row and inc one st at end of last row. 82(86,94) sts.

Change to 4.50 mm needles.

NOTE: DO NOT WEAVE colours when working in Fair Isle patt, but carry colour not in use loosely across on wrong side of work. Always carry colours to end of row. Darn in ends when making up.

Using MC, work 2 rows st st (1 row K, 1 row P).

**Using C1, work 2 rows st st.

Using MC, work 2 rows st st.

7th row: K2MC, * K2C2, K2MC, rep from * to end.

8th row: P2MC, * P2C2, P2MC, rep from * to end.

Work 6 rows st st, in stripes of 2 rows MC, 2 rows C3 and 2 rows MC.**

Beg patt

1st row: K2MC, * K2C1, K2MC, rep from * to end.

2nd row: P2MC, * P2C1, P2MC, rep from * to end.

Using MC, work 2 rows st st.

5th row: K2C2, * K2MC, K2C2, rep from * to end.

6th row: P2C2, * P2MC, P2C2, rep from * to end.

Using MC, work 2 rows st st.

9th row: K2MC, * K2C3, K2MC, rep from * to end.

10th row: P2MC, * P2C3, P2MC, rep from * to end.

Using MC, work 2 rows st st.

13th row: K2C1, * K2MC, K2C1, rep from * to end.

14th row: P2C1, * P2MC, P2C1, rep from * to end.

Using MC, work 2 rows st st.

17th row: K2MC, * K2C2, K2MC, rep from * to end.

18th row: P2MC, * P2C2, P2MC, rep from * to end.

Using MC, work 2 rows st st.

21st row: K2C3, * K2MC, K2C3, rep from * to end.

22nd row: P2C3, * P2MC, P2C3, rep from * to end.

Using MC, work 2 rows st st.

Last 24 rows form patt.

Cont in patt, dec 1 st at each end of next and foll 6th(10th,10th) rows until 70(78,86) sts rem, **2nd and 3rd sizes only** – then in foll 8th row/s until (76,82) sts rem.

Cont in patt without shaping until work measures approx 40(43,46) cm from beg, ending with MC and working last row on wrong side.

Shape armholes

Using C1, cast off 10(11,12) sts at beg of next 2 rows. 50(54,58) sts.

Using MC, work 2 rows st st.

5th row: K2C2, * K2MC, K2C2, rep from * to end.

6th row: P2C2, * P2MC, P2C2, rep from * to end.

MEASUREMENTS

To fit underarm	cm	41	46	51
	ins	16	18	20
Length to back neck				
	cm	49	53	57
Sleeve seam	cm	14	17	20

MATERIALS

Checkheaton 8 ply Machine Wash (50 g) balls (or other suitable 8 ply): 5(5,6) balls Main Colour (MC — Blue), 1(2,2) balls 1st Contrast (C1 — Yellow) 2 balls 2nd Contrast (C2 — Apricot), 1(1,2) ball/s 3rd Contrast (C3 — Aqua); 1 pair each 4.50 mm (No.7) and 3.25 mm (No. 10) knitting needles or the required size to give correct tension; 45(50,50) cm open ended zipper; 6 buttons; a stitch holder.

TENSION

22 sts to 10 cm over patt, using 4.50 mm needles.

It is important to knit a tension square and to work to the stated tension in order to obtain the required measurements. If your square is bigger use finer needles. If your square is smaller use thicker needles.

NOTE: This garment has been designed at a looser tension than normally recommended.

Using MC, work 2 rows st st.

Using C3, work 2 rows st st.

Using MC, work 2 rows st st, dec once in centre of last row. 49(53, 57) sts.

Proceed as follows

1st row: K0(0,2) MC, K0(1,1) C1, K1(2,2) MC, * K3C1, K2MC, K1C1, K1MC, K3C1, K5MC, K3C1, K1MC, K1C1, K2MC*, rep from * to * once, K3C1, K1(2,2) MC, K0(1,1) C1, K0(0,2) MC.

2nd row: P0(0,2) MC, P0(2,2) C1, P2MC, P1C1 *, P2MC, (P2C1, P2MC) twice, P1C1, P2MC, (P2C1, P2MC) twice P1C1*, rep from * to * once, P2MC, P0(2,2) C1, P0(0,2) MC.

Work rows 3 to 21 inclusive from Graph.

Using MC work 3 rows st st, inc one st in centre of last row.

50(54,58) sts.

Using C3 work 2 rows st st.

Using MC work 2 rows st st, **2nd and 3rd Sizes only —** Rep 5th and 6th rows as given in armhole shaping.

3rd Size only — Using MC work 4 rows st st.

Shape shoulders (all sizes)

Using MC only, cast off 8(9,9) sts at beg of next 2 rows, then 8(9,10) sts at beg of foll 2 rows.

Leave rem 18(18,20) sts on stitch holder.

LEFT FRONT

Using 3.25 mm needles and C2, cast on 41(43,49) sts.

Work 6 rows rib as for lower band of Back, inc (inc, dec) one st in centre of last row. 42(44,48) sts.

Change to 4.50 mm needles.

Using MC, work 2 rows st st.

Using C1, work 2 rows st st.

Using MC, work 2 rows st st. ***

7th row: * K2MC, K2C2, rep from * to last 2(0,0) sts, K2(0,0) MC.

8th row: P2(0, 0) MC, *P2C2, P2MC, rep from * to end.

Work 6 rows st st, in stripes of 2 rows MC, 2 rows C3 and 2 rows MC.

Beg patt

1st row: * K2MC, K2C1, rep from * to last 2(0,0) sts, K2(0,0) MC.

2nd row: P2(0,0) MC, *P2C1, P2MC, rep from * to end.

Work a further 22 rows patt (as for back) as placed in last 2 rows.

Cont in patt dec one st at beg of next and foll 6th(10th,10th) rows until 36(40,44) sts rem, **2nd and 3rd sizes only** – then in foll

Baby's Sleeping Bag

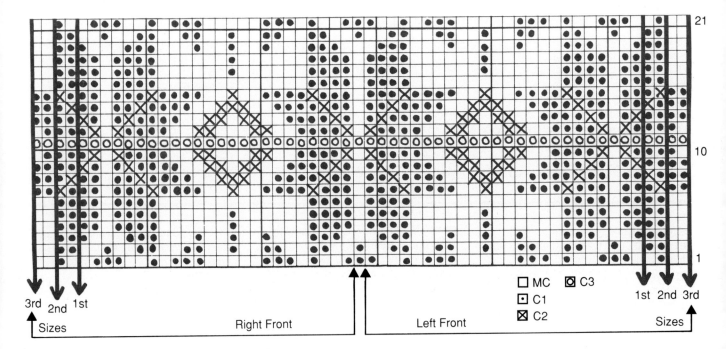

21

10

1

3rd 2nd 1st
Sizes

Right Front

Left Front

	MC	⊠	C3
⊡	C1	
⊠	C2	

1st 2nd 3rd
Sizes

8th rows until (39,42) sts rem.

Cont in patt without shaping until side edge measures 35(38,41) cm from beg, working last row on wrong side.

Shape armhole

Keeping patt correct, cast off 10(11,12) sts at beg of next row. 26(28,30) sts.

Work 11 rows patt as given for armhole shaping of Back, dec twice in centre of last row. 24(26,28) sts.

Next row: K0(0,2) MC, K0(1,1) C1, K1(2,2) MC, work as given from * to * on 1st row of Back, K1C1.

Next row: Work as given from * to * on 2nd row of Back, P2MC, P0(2,2) C1, P0(0,2) MC.

Work rows 3 to 15(15,19) inclusive from Graph.

Shape neck

Keeping patt correct, as from graph, cast off 4 sts at beg of next row. 20(22,24) sts.

Dec one st at neck edge in next row and foll alt rows 2(2,0) times, thus completing graph. 17(19,23) sts.

Cont in patt as for Back, dec one st at neck edge in alt row/s until 16(18,19) sts rem. Work 5(7,5) rows patt.

Shape shoulder

Cast off 8(9,9) sts at beg of next row.
Work 1 row. Cast off.

RIGHT FRONT

Work as for Left Front to ***.

7th row: K2(0,2) MC, * K2C2, K2MC, rep from * to end.

8th row: * P2MC, P2C2, rep from * to last

2(0,2) sts, P2(0,2) MC.

Complete to correspond with Left Front.

SLEEVES

Using 3.25 mm needles and C1, cast on 31(33,35) sts.

Work as given for lower band of Back until band measures 4 cm from beg, ending with a 1st row.

Next row: Inc once in each st to end. 62(66,70) sts.

Change to 4.50 mm needles and MC.

Work in patt (as for Back), until work measures approx 13(16,19) cm from beg, ending with a purl row in MC.

Tie a coloured thread at ends of last row.

Work as given from ** to ** on Back.

Using MC, work 2(4,6) rows st st.

Shape top

Cast off 8 sts at beg of next 6 rows.
Cast off rem sts.

NECKBAND

Using back stitch, join shoulder seams. With right side facing, using 3.25 mm needles and MC, knit up 53(57,59) sts evenly around neck (including sts from stitch holder).

Work in rib as for lower band of Back, beg with a 2nd row, until neckband measures 3 cm from beg, ending with a 2nd row.
Cast off loosely in rib.

TO MAKE UP

Press lightly on wrong side, using damp cloth and cool iron. Using back stitch, join side and sleeve seams to coloured threads.

Sew in sleeves, placing rows above coloured thread to sts cast off at underarm. Sew in zip. Fold back lower edge onto right side. Sew on buttons to correspond with buttonholes.

FAIR ISLE

Fair Isle is a small island off the coast of Scotland, which has given its name to a very easily recognisable coloured knitting pattern.

Local legend has it that the colours and intricate patterns were based on those worn by Spanish sailors shipwrecked on the island after the defeat of the Spanish Armada in 1588. Others hold that the patterns were handed down by Viking explorers from Scandinavia.

A true Fair Isle pattern usually had two colours to a row and used a Shetland wool called "fingering". In the past the lovely colours of Fair Isle were dyed with natural dyes. These days chemical dyes are used to reproduce traditional colours. Classic Fair Isle patterns have been repeated unchanged for generations.

STRIPE TRIM
SHEET

This sheet is made in exactly the same manner as the spot-trimmed sheet on page 23. We have trimmed a plain cotton with a pretty pattern in toning shades of cream and apricot. The bias trim can be in a complementary or contrasting colour.

CREAM SLEEPSUIT

Make this cosy sleepsuit, following the instructions for the striped suit on page 23. We have used stretch towelling, trimmed with bias made from the cot bumper fabric. This is the ideal fabric for baby's comfort and so easy to care for.

COT BUMPER

MATERIALS
The quantity of fabric will depend on the size of your cot.

☐ one piece the width of the cot by twice the distance from the mattress to the top rail; two pieces two thirds the length of the cot by twice the distance from the mattress to the top rail

☐ scraps of fabric, ribbon or doubled bias binding for ties

☐ thin wadding (batting) in same sizes as fabric

1   Tack wadding to wrong side of each fabric piece. Fold each piece over double with right sides together. Sew around edges, leaving opening for turning. Turn to right side. Close opening by hand.

2   Make 12 ties each 80 cm x 2 cm. Stitch centre of each tie to each corner of three bumper sections. Topstitch all around each bumper section.

Above top: Stripe Trim Sheet, Cot Bumper; Above: Cream Sleepsuit

Lavender and Lace

You can almost smell the lavender! Knit or sew a family heirloom with these all-time favourites. Team the lacy layette in snowy white with the prettiest lavender, crisp green and white patchwork quilt, that's so easy to make, and an embroidered nightie in gossamer voile.

JACKET, BONNET AND BOOTEES

JACKET
BACK
Using 3 mm needles, cast on 146(162,178) sts.

Work 3 rows garter st – every row K (1st row is wrong side).

Beg patt

1st row: P2, *K4, K2tog, yrn, P2, rep from * to end.

2nd row: K2, * yrn, Pl, P2tog, P3, K2, rep from * to end.

3rd row: P2, *K2, K2tog, K2, yrn, P2, rep from * to end.

4th row: K2, * yrn, P3, P2tog, Pl, K2, rep from * to end.

5th row: P2, *K2tog, K4, yrn, P2, rep from * to end.

6th row: K2, *P4, P2tog, yon, K2, rep from * to end.

7th row: P2, * yon, Kl, K2tog, K3, P2, rep from * to end.

8th row: K2, *P2, P2tog, P2, yon, K2, rep from * to end.

9th row: P2, * yon, K3, K2tog, Kl, P2, rep from * to end.

10th row: K2, *P2tog, P4, yon, K2, rep from * to end.

Rows 1 to 10 inclusive form patt.

Cont in patt until work measures 16.5(18,21) cm from beg, working last row on wrong side.

Next row: Kl, *K2tog, rep from * to last st, Kl. 74(82,90) sts.

Next row: Purl.

Next row: K2(1,2), * yfwd, K2tog, Kl, rep from * to last 0(0,1) st/s, K0(01).

Work 3 rows st st (1 row K, 1 row P), beg with a purl row.

Shape armholes

Cast off 4(4,5) sts at beg of next 2 rows.

Dec 1 st at each end of next and alt rows until 60(66,72) sts rem.

Work 31(31,35) rows.

Shape shoulders

Cast off 10(11,12) sts at beg of next 2 rows, then 9(10,11) sts at beg of foll 2 rows.

Leave rem 22(24,26) sts on a stitch holder.

LEFT FRONT
Using 3 mm needles, cast on 80(88,96)

MEASUREMENTS

To fit underarm			
cm	41	46	51
ins	16	18	20
Actual measurement			
cm	45	50	55
Length to back neck			
cm	27	29	33
Sleeve seam cm	12.5	15	18

MATERIALS
Cleckheaton Babysoft 3 ply (25 g) balls (or other suitable 3ply): 4(4,5) balls for Jacket, 1 ball each for Bonnet and Bootees; 1 pair each 3 mm (No. 11) and 2.25 mm (No. 13) knitting needles or the required size to give correct tension; 3 stitch holders for Jacket; length of ribbon.

ABBREVIATIONS
"MI" = Pick up loop which lies before next st, place on left hand needle, and knit through back of loop.

TENSION
32 sts to 10 cm over stocking st, using 3 mm needles.

It is important to knit a tension square and to work to the stated tension in order to obtain the required measurements. If your square is bigger use finer needles. If your square is smaller use thicker needles.

sts.

Work 3 rows garter st (1st row is wrong side). **

Beg patt

1st row: P2, * K4, K2tog, yrn, P2, rep from * to last 6 sts, K6.

2nd row: K6, * K2 yrn, Pl, P2tog, P3, rep from * to last 2 sts, K2.

Cont in patt as for Back (keeping garter st border correct as placed in last 2 rows) until work measures 16.5(18,21) cm from beg, working last row on wrong side.

Next row: * K2tog, rep from * to last 6 sts, K6. 43(47,51) sts.

Next row: K6, purl to end.

Next row: K1(2,0), * Kl, yfwd, K2tog, rep from * to last 6 sts, K6.

Cont in st st, keeping garter st border correct, work 3 rows (beg with a purl row).

Shape armhole

Cast off 4(4,5) sts at beg of next row.

Dec 1 st at armhole edge in alt rows until

36(39,42) sts rem.

Work 16(16,18) rows.

Shape neck

1st row: Patt 11(12,12) sts and slip them onto a stitch holder, purl to end.

Cont on these 25(27, 30) sts.

Dec 1 st at end (neck edge) of next and alt rows until 19(21,23) sts rem.

Work 3 rows.

Shape shoulder

Cast off 10(11,12) sts at beg of next row.

Work 1 row.

Cast off.

RIGHT FRONT
Work as for Left Front to **.

Beg patt

1st row: K6, P2, *K4, K2tog, yrn, P2, rep from * to end.

2nd row: K2, * yrn, Pl, P2tog, P3, K2, rep from * to last 6 sts, K6.

Complete to correspond with Left Front.

SLEEVES
Using 2.25 mm needles, cast on 43(45,47) sts.

1st row: K2, *Pl, Kl, rep from * to last st, Kl.

2nd row: Kl, *Pl, Kl, rep from * to end.

Rep 1st and 2nd rows 6 times.

Change to 3 mm needles.

Next row: K6(5,2), *inc in next st, Kl, rep from * to last 5(4,1) st/s, K5(4,1). 59(63,69) sts.

Cont in st st (beg with a purl row) until work measures 12.5(15,18) cm from beg, ending with a purl row.

Shape top

Cast off 2(2,3) sts at beg of next 2 rows.

Dec 1 st at each end of next and alt rows until 47(51,55) sts rem, then in every row until 13 sts rem.

Cast off.

NECKBAND
Using back stitch, join shoulder seams. With right side facing and using 2.25 mm needles, knit up 72(78,84) sts evenly around neck (including sts from stitch holders).

1st row (wrong side): Knit.

2nd row: K6, * Kl, y fwd, K2tog, rep from * to last 6 sts, K6.

Knit 5 rows.

Cast off.

TO MAKE UP
Press very lightly with a cool iron on wrong side if desired. Using back stitch, join side and sleeve seams. Sew in sleeves. Thread ribbon through holes at underarm and neck, as illustrated.

BONNET

Using 2.25 mm needles, cast on 90(98,106) sts.

Work 5 rows garter st (1st row is wrong side).

Change to 3 mm needles.

Work 12 rows st st.

Work 20 rows patt, as for Back of Jacket.

Cont in stocking st until work measures 12(13, 14) cm from beg, ending with a purl row.

Shape crown

1st row: Kl, * K2tog, K9(10,11), rep from * to last st, Kl. 82(90,98) sts.

2nd and alt rows: Kl, purl to last st, Kl.

3rd row: Kl, *K2tog, K8(9, 10), rep from * to last st, K1. 74(82,90) sts.

5th row: Kl, *K2tog, K7(8,9), rep from * to last st, K1. 66(74,82) sts.

Cont dec in this manner in alt rows until 10 sts rem.

Break off yarn, run end through rem sts, draw up and fasten off securely.

LOWER BAND

Using a flat seam, join crown seam.

With right side facing and using 2.25 mm needles, knit up 68(72,76) sts evenly around lower edge.

Work 3 rows garter st.

Cast off.

TO MAKE UP

Attach ribbons to each side and tie, as illustrated.

BOOTEES

Using 3 mm needles, cast on 35(39,43) sts.

1st row: Kl, "M1". K16(18,20), "Ml", Kl, "Ml", K16(18,20), "Ml", K1 (1st row is wrong side). 39(43,47) sts.

2nd and alt rows: Knit.

3rd row: Kl, "M1", K18(20, 22), "Ml", Kl, "Ml", K18(20,22), "Ml", Kl. 43(47,51) sts.

5th row: K1, "M1", K20(22,24), "M1", K1, "M1", K20(22,24), "M1", K1. 47(51,55) sts.

Inc in this manner in alt rows until there are 59(63,67) sts.

Next row: K2tog, knit to last 2 sts, K2tog.

Shawl, Jacket and Bonnet

57(61,65) sts.
Work 5(7,11) rows garter st.
Shape instep
1st row: K33(35,37), K2tog tbl, TURN.
2nd row: Sl1, P9, P2tog, TURN.
3rd row: Sl1, K9, K2tog tbl,TURN.
4th row: Sl1, P9, P2tog, TURN.
Rep 3rd and 4th rows until 37(41,45) sts rem.
Next row: Sl1, K9, K2tog tbl, knit to end. 36(40,44) sts.
Next row: Knit across all sts to end.
Next row: Kl, * yfwd, K2tog, rep from * to last st, Kl.

Next row: Knit, inc 6(2,6) sts evenly across row. 42(42,50) sts.
Work 20 rows patt as for Back of Jacket, dec (inc, dec) 1 st in centre of last row. 41(43,49) sts. Change to 2.25 mm needles and work 8 rows rib as for Sleeves of Jacket.
Cast off loosely in rib.

TO MAKE UP
Do not press.
Using a flat seam, join foot and back seam. Thread narrow ribbon through holes and tie into bow.

BABY'S SHAWL

CENTRE
Using 3 mm needles, cast on 224 sts.
1st row: * P1, K1, rep from * to end.
2nd row: * K1, P1, rep from * to end.
Last 2 rows form Moss Stitch.
Rep 1st and 2nd rows 4 times, dec 12 sts evenly across last row (noting not to dec across 10 sts at each end). 212 sts.
Beg centre patt
1st row: (P1, K1) 5 times, * K3, yfwd, sl1, K2tog, psso, yfwd, rep from * to last 10 sts, (P1, K1) 5 times.
2nd row: (K1, P1) 5 times, purl to last 10 sts, (K1, P1) 5 times.
3rd row: (P1, K1) 5 times, * yfwd, sl1 K2tog, psso, yfwd, K3, rep from * to last 10 sts, (P1, K1) 5 times.
4th row: As 2nd row.
Rows 1 to 4 inclusive form patt.
Cont in patt until work measures 64 cm

MEASUREMENT
Approx 137 cm square.

MATERIALS
Cleckheaton Babysoft 3 ply (25 g) balls (or other suitable 3 ply): 20 balls; 1 pair of 3 mm (No. 11) knitting needles or the required size to give correct tension.

TENSION
30 sts to 10 cm over centre patt, using 3 mm needles and 32 sts to 10 cm over st st, using 3 mm needles.
It is important to knit a tension square and to work to the stated tension in order to obtain the required measurements. If your square is bigger use finer needles. If your square is smaller use thicker needles.

from beg, working last row on wrong side and inc 12 sts evenly across last row (noting not to inc across 10 sts at each end). 224 sts.
Work 10 rows Moss Stitch.
Cast off loosely.
BORDER (make 4)
With right side facing, using 3 mm needles, knit up 213 sts evenly along side edge of centre.
Knit one row, working into the back of each st.
Begin Patt
1st row: K2, yfwd, K2tog, * yfwd, K5, yfwd, sl1, K2tog, psso, rep from * to last 9 sts, yfwd, K5, yfwd, sl1, K1, psso, yfwd, K2. 215 sts.
2nd row: K2, inc in next st, purl to last 3 sts, inc in next st, K2. 217 sts.
3rd row: K2, yfwd, K1, * yfwd, sl1, K2tog,

psso, yfwd, K5, rep from * to last 6 sts, yfwd, sl1, K2tog, psso, yfwd, K1, yfwd, K2. 219 sts.
4th row: K2, purl to last 2 sts, K2.
5th row: K2, yfwd, K2tog, * yfwd, K3, yfwd, sl1, K1, psso, K1, K2tog, rep from * to last 7 sts, yfwd, K3, yfwd, sl1, K1, psso, yfwd, K2. 221 sts.
6th row: As 2nd row. 223 sts.
7th row: K2, yfwd, K1, K2tog, * yfwd, K1, yfwd, sl1, K2tog, psso, rep from * to last 6 sts, yfwd, K1, yfwd, sl1, K1, psso, K1, yfwd, K2. 225 sts.
8th row: As 4th row.
9th row: K2, * yfwd, K5, yfwd, sl1, K2tog, psso, rep from * to last 7 sts, yfwd, K5, yfwd, K2. 227 sts.
10th row: As 2nd row. 229 sts.
11th row: As 1st row. 231 sts.
12th row: As 4th row.
13th row: K2, * yfwd, K3, yfwd, sl1, K1, psso, K1, K2tog, rep from * to last 5 sts, yfwd, K3, yfwd, K2. 233 sts.
14th row: As 2nd row. 235 sts.
15th row: K2, yfwd, K2, * yfwd, sl1, K2tog, psso, yfwd, K1, rep from * to last 3 sts, K1, yfwd, K2. 237 sts.
16th row: As 4th row.
17th row: K2, yfwd, K3, * yfwd, sl1, K2tog, psso, yfwd, K5, rep from * to last 8 sts, yfwd, sl1, K2tog, psso, yfwd, K3, yfwd, K2. 239 sts.
18th row: As 2nd row. 241 sts.
19th row: As 9th row. 243 sts.
20th row: As 4th row.
21st row: K2, yfwd, K1, * yfwd, sl1, K1, psso, K1, K2tog, yfwd, K3, rep from * to last 7 sts, yfwd, sl1, K1, psso, K1, K2tog, yfwd, K1, yfwd, K2. 245 sts.
22nd row: As 2nd row. 247 sts.
23rd row: K2, yfwd, K1, K2tog, * yfwd, K1, yfwd, sl1, K2tog, psso, rep from * to last 6

sts, yfwd, K1, yfwd, sl1, K1, psso, K1, yfwd, K2. 249 sts.

24th row: As 4th row.
25th row: As 3rd row. 251 sts.
26th row: As 2nd row. 253 sts.
27th row: As 17th row. 255 sts.
28th row: As 4th row.
29th row: K2, yfwd, K2, * K2tog, yfwd, K3, yfwd, sl1, K1, psso, K1, rep from * to last 3 sts, K1, yfwd, K2. 257 sts.
30th row: As 2nd row. 259 sts.
31st row: As 15th row. 261 sts.
32nd row: As 4th row.

Rep rows 1 to 32 inclusive twice, then rows 1 to 8 inclusive once, dec one st at end of last row. 368 sts.

Cont in Moss Stitch, inc one st at each end of 2nd row, then in foll 4th rows until there are 374 sts.

Cast off loosely.

TO MAKE UP

Using a flat seam, join edges of Borders. With a slightly damp cloth and warm iron press lightly.

PATCHWORK QUILT

MATERIALS

☐ 30 cm of 115 cm wide cream cotton fabric
☐ 1.5 m of 115 cm wide green cotton fabric for strips, binding and backing
☐ 70 cm of 115 cm wide floral print fabric
☐ 60 cm of 115 cm wide lavender cotton fabric
☐ piece of wadding (batting) 115 cm x 78 cm

NOTE: Some quilters add length to cut strips to allow for fabric movement while stitching.

Join all pieces together with right sides facing. 1 cm seams allowed.

1   Make strips of all four fabrics 6 cm wide and 4.40 m long. Sew strips together lengthways. Press seams open. Cut length into twenty four pieces each 18 cm square.
2   Sew squares together in pattern as shown. Sew 6 cm wide strips of lavender fabric down each side, then across both ends. Sew 10 cm wide strips of floral fabric down both sides, then across each end.
3   Place quilt top and backing together, with wrong sides facing and wadding in between. Tack together around edges.
4   Stitch around each square and along edges of borders through all thicknesses.
5   Bind edges of quilt using strips of green fabric.

NAPPY PIN CUSHION

MATERIALS

☐ remnants of four cotton print fabrics
☐ polyester fibre for stuffing

1   Make two squares as for patchwork quilt.
2   Place together with right sides facing. Stitch around outside edge, leaving small opening for turning. Turn and stuff firmly. Close opening by hand.

Left: Nappy Pin Cushion
Below: Patchwork Quilt

EMBROIDERED NIGHTIE

SIZE: 0 to 6 months

MATERIALS
- ☐ 1.5 m of 115 cm wide fine cotton voile
- ☐ three small buttons
- ☐ 2 m of 3 cm wide cotton lace
- ☐ 3 m of 1 cm wide lace for hem
- ☐ embroidery thread

PATTERN
Pattern outline ○━●━○━●━○━●━○━●━○━●━○
1 front yoke (cut 2); 2 back yoke (cut 2); 3 front/back skirt (cut 2); 4 sleeves (cut 2) Cut out pattern pieces as directed. 1 cm seams allowed. Slit nightie back for 8 cm down from top edge. Use narrow French seams to join side, centre, sleeve and armhole seams. For a firmer yoke, interface with lightest possible interfacing.

1 Sew sleeves into armholes edges of front and back skirts. Sew side seams from wrists to hem. Press. Neaten edges of skirt back opening.

2 Fold under 6 cm at hem, twice. Press. Machine stitch hem into place and again along fold. Stitch 1 cm wide lace over both rows of stitching.

3 Press under 6 mm at wrists and again 1 cm. Stitch with double row to form casing, leaving opening for elastic. Stitch wider lace just under wrist edge. Insert elastic, secure ends and close opening.

4 Sew shoulder seams of yokes and of yoke facings. Fold back yoke extension (facing) to outside along foldline, placing yoke and facing with right sides together. Sew around neck edge, matching neck edges. Trim seam, clip curves. Turn facing to inside. Press.

5 Press centre back opening edges to inside along foldline.

6 Gather skirt as far as centre back opening. Pin slightly gathered lace around skirt along gathering line. Pin nightie to yoke, adjusting gathering to fit and taking care to keep yoke facing free. Stitch. Press seam towards yoke.

7 Press under raw edge on yoke facing. Slipstitch over previous stitching. On outside, edgestitch around all edges of yoke.

8 Make buttonholes. Sew on buttons.

9 Embroider grub roses following instructions opposite.

HOW TO EMBROIDER
GRUB ROSES

Grub roses are stitched in toning shades of stranded cotton, starting with darkest shade at centre and working out to lightest shade. Stitch leaves in bullion knots or chain stitch in tones of green.

Bring needle up at A. Take a stitch from B to A; do not pull needle through (A to B equals the width of knot required). Twist thread several times around the needle clockwise covering width of AB. Pull needle through easing twisted thread onto fabric. Re-insert needle at B. Build up bullion knots as shown below.

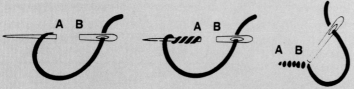

EMBROIDERED FACE CLOTH

Make a purchased face cloth into a very special one by embroidering a border of grub roses as shown, following the instructions above.

Using the same technique, you can add your personal touch to sheets, towels or a simple baby's cotton vest.

BABY'S BATHTIME

When preparing your baby's bath, make sure that you have everything you will need, such as soap, face cloth and towel, within easy reach. Plan the area around the bath with easy access to storage shelves, changing table and baby's clothes. A nursery basket or box, lined with some pretty, washable fabric is ideal for holding all those bits and pieces like talc, nappy pins and a pin cushion, and some very special soap.

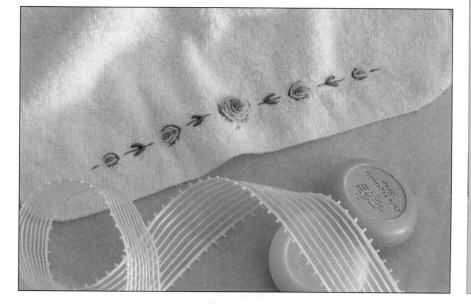

BABY'S DRESS

MEASUREMENTS

To fit underarm	cm	46
	ins	18
Actual measurement approx		
	cm	49
Length to back neck		
	cm	48
Sleeve seam	cm	5

MATERIALS

Cleckheaton Babysoft 3 ply (25 g) (or other suitable 3 ply); 5 balls; 1 pair each of 3 mm (No. 11) and 2.25 mm (No. 13) knitting needles or the required size to give correct tension; a 3 mm (No. 10-11) crochet hook; 3 buttons.

TENSION

32 sts to 10 cm over st st, using 3 mm needles.

It is important to knit a tension square and to work to the stated tension in order to obtain the required measurements. If your square is bigger use finer needles. If your square is smaller use thicker needles.

FRONT

Using 3 mm needles, cast on 140 sts.
Work 9 rows in garter st (every row knit – 1st row is wrong side).
Work 2 rows st st (1 row K, 1 row P).

Beg patt

1st row: K14, * yfwd, sl1, K1, psso, K20, rep from * ending last rep with K14, instead of K20.

2nd and alt rows: Purl.

3rd row: K12, * K2tog, yfwd, K1, yfwd, sl1, K1, psso, K17, rep from * ending last rep with K13, instead of K17.

5th row: K11, * K2tog, yfwd, sl1, K2tog, psso, yfwd, sl1, K1, psso, K15, rep from * ending last rep with K12, instead of K15.

7th row: K13, * yfwd, K1, yfwd, K19, rep from * ending last rep with K14, instead of K19.

9th row: K25, * yfwd, sl1, K1, psso, K20, rep from * ending last rep with K25, instead of K20.

11th row: K23, * K2tog, yfwd, K1, yfwd, sl1, K1, psso, K17, rep from * ending last rep with K24, instead of K17.

13th row: K22, * K2tog, yfwd, sl1, K2tog, psso, yfwd, sl1, K1, psso, K15, rep from * ending last rep with K23, instead of K15.

15th row: K24, * yfwd, K1, yfwd, K19, rep from * ending last rep with K25, instead of K19.

17th row: K25, * yfwd, K2tog, K20, rep from * ending last rep with K25, instead of K20.

18th row: Purl.

Rep 17th and 18th rows until work measures 15 cm from beg, ending with a purl row.

Dec row: K12, K2tog, K11, * yfwd, K2tog, K9, K2tog, K9, rep from * until 27 sts rem, yfwd, K2tog, K11, K2tog, K12. 134 sts.

Next row: Purl.

Next row: K24, * yfwd, K2tog, K19, rep from * ending with K24, instead of K19.

Next row: Purl.

Rep last 2 rows until work measures 17.5 cm from beg, ending with a purl row.

Dec row: K11, K2tog, K11, * yfwd, K2tog, K8, K2tog, K9, rep from * until 26 sts rem, yfwd, K2tog, K11, K2tog, K11. 128 sts.

Next row: Purl.

Next row: K23, * yfwd, K2tog, K18, rep from * ending last rep with K23, instead of K18.

Next row: Purl.

Rep last 2 rows until work measures 20 cm from beg, ending with a purl row.

Dec row: K10, K2tog, K11, * yfwd, K2tog, K8, K2tog, K8, rep from * until 25 sts rem, yfwd, K2tog, K10, K2tog, K11. 122 sts.

Next row: Purl.

Next row: K22, * yfwd, K2tog, K17, rep from * ending last rep with K22, instead of K17.

Next row: Purl.

Rep last 2 rows until work measures 22.5 cm from beg, ending with a purl row.

Dec row: K10, K2tog, K10, * yfwd, K2tog, K7, K2tog, K8, rep from * until 24 sts rem, yfwd, K2tog, K10, K2tog, K10. 116 sts.

Next row: Purl.

Next row: K21, * yfwd, K2tog, K16, rep from * until 23 sts rem, yfwd, K2tog, K21.

Next row: Purl.

Rep last 2 rows until work measures 25 cm from beg, ending with a purl row.

Dec row: K8, K2tog, K1, K2tog, K8, * yfwd, K2tog, K5, K2tog, K1, K2tog, K6, rep from * until 23 sts rem, yfwd, K2tog, K8, K2tog, K1, K2tog, K8. 104 sts.

Next row: Purl.

Next row: K19, * yfwd, K2tog, K14, rep from * ending last rep with K19, instead of K14.

Next row: Purl.

Rep last 2 rows until work measures 27.5 cm from beg, ending with a purl row.

Dec row: K7, K2tog, K1, K2tog, K7, * yfwd, K2tog, K4, K2tog, K1, K2tog, K5, rep from * until 21 sts rem, yfwd, K2tog, K7, K2tog, K1, K2tog, K7. 92 sts.

Next row: Purl. **

Commence yoke

1st row: K17, yfwd, K2tog, K12, yfwd, K2tog, K10, K2tog, yfwd, K1, yfwd, sl1, K1, psso, K11, yfwd, K2tog, K12, yfwd, K2tog, K17.

2nd and alt rows: Purl.

3rd row: K17, yfwd, K2tog, K12, yfwd, K2tog, K9, K2tog, yfwd, K3, yfwd, sl1, K1, psso, K10, yfwd, K2tog, K12, yfwd, K2tog, K17.

5th row: K17, yfwd, K2tog, K12, yfwd, K2tog, K8, K2tog, yfwd, K5, yfwd, sl1, K1, psso, K9, yfwd, K2tog, K12, yfwd, K2tog, K17.

7th row: K6, K2tog, K1, K2tog, K6, yfwd, K2tog, K3, K2tog, K1, K2tog, K4, yfwd, K2tog, K3, K2tog, K2, K2tog, yfwd, K3, yfwd, sl1, K1, psso, K2, yfwd, sl1, K1, psso K3, K2tog, K3, yfwd, K2tog, K4, K2tog, K1, K2tog, K3, yfwd, K2tog, K7, K2tog, K1, K2tog, K5. 82 sts.

9th row: K15, yfwd, K2tog, K10, yfwd, K2tog, K5, K2tog, yfwd, K2, K2tog, yfwd, K1, yfwd, sl1, K1, psso, K2, yfwd, sl1, K1, psso, K6, yfwd, K2tog, K10, yfwd, K2tog, K15.

11th row: K15, yfwd, K2tog, K10, yfwd, K2tog, K4, K2tog, yfwd, K2, K2tog, yfwd, sl1, K2tog, psso, yfwd, sl1, K1, psso, K2, yfwd, sl1, K1, psso, K5, yfwd, K2tog, K10, yfwd, K2tog, K15.

13th row: K15, yfwd, K2tog, K10, yfwd, K2tog, K3, K2tog, yfwd, K5, yfwd, K1, yfwd, K5, yfwd, sl1, K1, psso, K4, yfwd, K2tog, K10, yfwd, K2tog, K15.

14th row: Purl.

Shape armholes

15th row: Cast off 3 sts, K3 (this includes st left on right hand needle from cast-off), (K2tog) twice, K5, yfwd, K2tog, K3, (K2tog) twice, K3, yfwd, K2tog, K2, K2tog, yfwd, K3, yfwd, sl1, K1, psso, K6, yfwd, sl1, K1, psso, K2, yfwd, sl1, K1, psso, K3, yfwd, K2tog, K3, (K2tog) twice, K3, yfwd, K2tog, K5, (K2tog) twice, K6.

16th row: Cast off 3 sts, purl to end. 68 sts.

17th row: K2tog, (K8, yfwd, K2tog) twice, K1, K2tog, yfwd, K2, K2tog, yfwd, K1, yfwd, sl1, K1, psso, K3, K2tog, yfwd, K1, yfwd, sl1, K1, psso, K2, yfwd, sl1, K1, psso, K2, (yfwd, K2tog, K8) twice, K2tog.

18th row: P2tog, purl to last 2 sts, P2tog.

19th row: K2tog, K6, yfwd, K2tog, K8, yfwd, (K2tog) twice, yfwd, K2, K2tog, yfwd, sl1, K2tog, psso, yfwd, sl1, K1, psso, K1, K2tog, yfwd, sl1, K2tog, psso, yfwd, sl1, K1, psso, K2, yfwd, sl1, K1, psso, K1, yfwd, K2tog, K8, yfwd, K2tog, K6, K2tog.

20th row: P2tog, purl to last 2 sts, P2tog. 60 sts.

21st row: K6, yfwd, K2tog, K8, yfwd, K3tog, yfwd, (K5, yfwd, K1, yfwd) twice, K5, yfwd, sl1, K1, psso, yfwd, K2tog, K8, yfwd, K2tog, K6.

22nd and alt rows: Purl.

23rd row: K6, yfwd, K2tog, K8, K2tog, yfwd, K3, yfwd, sl1, K1, psso, K14, yfwd, sl1, K1, psso, K2, yfwd, sl1, K1, psso, K9, yfwd, K2tog, K6.

25th row: K6, yfwd, K2tog, K7, K2tog, yfwd, K2, K2tog, yfwd, K1, yfwd, sl1, K1, psso, K11, K2tog, yfwd, K1, yfwd, sl1, K1, psso, K2, yfwd, sl1, K1, psso, K8, yfwd, K2tog, K6.

27th row: K6, yfwd, K2tog, K6, K2tog, yfwd, K2, K2tog, yfwd, sl1, K2tog, psso, yfwd, sl1, K1, psso, K9, K2tog, yfwd, sl1, K2tog, psso, yfwd, sl1, K1, psso, K2, yfwd, sl1, K1, psso, K7, yfwd, K2tog, K6.

29th row: K6, yfwd, K2tog, K5, K2tog, yfwd, K5, yfwd, K1, yfwd, K13, yfwd, K1, yfwd, K5, yfwd, sl1, K1, psso, K6, yfwd, K2tog, K6.

Keeping patt correct, work a further 7 rows.

Shape neck

37th row: K6, yfwd, K2tog, K1, K2tog, yfwd, K5, yfwd, K1, yfwd, K3, cast off next

16 sts, K2 (this includes st left on right hand needle from cast-off), yfwd, K1, yfwd, K5, yfwd, sl1, K1, psso, K2, yfwd, K2tog, K6.

Keeping patt correct, cont on last 22 sts, dec one st at neck edge in every row 4 times. 18 sts.

42nd row: Purl.

43rd row: K2tog, yfwd, sl1, K2tog, psso, yfwd, sl1, K1, psso, K2, yfwd, sl1, K1, psso, K7.

Keeping patt correct, work a further 6 rows.

Cast off.

Join yarn at neck edge and complete other side of neck to correspond.

BACK

Work as for Front to **.

Next row: K17, * yfwd, K2tog, K12, rep from * until 19 sts rem, yfwd, K2tog, K17.

Next row: Purl.

Rep last 2 rows twice.

Dec row: K6, K2tog, K1, K2tog, K6, yfwd, K2tog, K3, K2tog, K1, K2tog, K4, yfwd, K2tog, (K5, K2tog, K5, yfwd, K2tog) twice, K3, K2tog, K1, K2tog, K4, yfwd, K2tog, K6, K2tog, K1, K2tog, K6. 82 sts.

Next row: Purl.

Next row: K15, yfwd, K2tog, K10, yfwd, K2tog, (K11, yfwd, K2tog twice), K10, yfwd, K2tog, K15.

Next row: Purl.

Divide for back opening

Next row: K15, yfwd, K2tog, K10, yfwd, K2tog, K9, turn, cast on 6 sts for underlap. Cont on last 44 sts.

Next row: K6, purl to end.

Next row: K15, yfwd, K2tog, K10, yfwd, K2tog, K15.

Next row: K6, purl to end.

Shape armhole
Next row: Cast off 3 sts, K3 (this includes st left on right hand needle from cast-off), (K2tog) twice, K5, yfwd, K2tog, K3, (K2tog) twice, K3, yfwd, K2tog, K15. 37 sts.
Next row: K6, purl to end.
Next row: K2tog, K8, yfwd, K2tog, K8, yfwd, K2tog, K15.
Next row: K6, purl to last 2 sts, P2tog. 35 sts.
Next row: K2tog, K6, yfwd, K2tog, K8, yfwd, K2tog, K15.
Next row: K6, purl to last 2 sts, P2tog. 33 sts.
Keeping patt correct, cont until there are 3 rows less than Front to Shoulder shaping.
Shape back neck
Keeping patt correct, cast off 13 sts, purl to end.
Dec one st at neck edge in every row twice. 18 sts.
Cast off.
Join yarn to rem sts and proceed as follows:
Next row: K15, yfwd, K2tog, K10, yfwd, K2tog, K15.

Next row: Purl to last 6 sts, K6.
Next row: K3, yfwd, K2tog (buttonhole), K10, yfwd, K2tog, K10, yfwd, K2tog, K15.
Next row: Purl to last 6 sts, K6.
Next row: K15, yfwd, K2tog, K3, (K2tog) twice, K3, yfwd, K2tog, K5, (K2tog) twice, K6.
Complete to correspond with other side, working 2 more buttonholes as before evenly along back opening and noting to begin armhole shaping on next row.
SLEEVES
Using 2.25 mm needles, cast on 42 sts.
Work 7 rows garter st (1st row is wrong side).
Change to 3 mm needles.
Next row: K2, * knit into next st, twice, K1, rep from * to end. 62 sts.
Next row: Purl.
Beg patt
1st row: K5, * yfwd, sl1, K1, psso, K8, rep from * ending last rep with K5, instead of K8.
2nd and alt rows: Purl.
3rd row: K3, * K2tog, yfwd, K1, yfwd, sl1, K1, psso, K5, rep from * ending last rep

with K4, instead of K5.
5th row: K2, * K2tog, yfwd, sl1, K2tog, psso, yfwd, sl1, K1, psso, K3, rep from * to end.
7th row: K4, * yfwd, K1, yfwd, K7, rep from * ending last rep with K5, instead of K7.
8th row: Purl.
Cont in st st until work measures 5 cm from beg, ending with a purl row.
Shape top
Dec one st at each end of every row until 18 sts rem.
Cast off.

TO MAKE UP
Using back stitch, join shoulder, side and sleeve seams. Sew in sleeves, easing extra fullness across top of sleeve. Sew underlap in position at back opening. Using 3 mm crochet hook, work one row of dc evenly around neck edge, having a number divisible by three plus one.
Next round: 1ch, * 1dc into each of next 3dc, 3ch, slip st back into first of these 3ch, rep from * to last dc, 1dc in last dc. Fasten off. Sew on buttons.

FLORAL BUNNY

Make this nursery charmer in exactly the same way as the bunny on page 15.

♡ HINT ♡

Choose trims of the same fabric you are sewing to prevent problems when washing and ironing. A synthetic trim on a cotton sheet may well dissolve under a hot iron while an iron on a cooler setting won't do the job. Keep this in mind when choosing ribbons, binding and motifs as well as lace.

BRODERIE ANGLAISE SHEETS

MATERIALS
- ☐ 150 cm of 115 cm wide broderie cotton
- ☐ 120 cm wide broderie lace
- ☐ 1.5 m narrow satin ribbon.

1 Sew broderie lace to top edge of sheet with right sides together. Finish raw edges of seam as desired. Stitch ribbon over seam and tie in bow at centre.
2 Hem all raw edges of sheet.

50

NURSERY BASICS

Your baby's nursery will be a special place for the two of you to share. With a little imagination, some planning and not a great deal of money, you can turn a small room or even a dull corner into a pretty haven. There are some basic elements you will need to provide.

☐ Bassinet or cot
New babies sleep best in a reasonably confined, cosy space, but soon outgrow this. You will need to make your own decision as to when your baby moves to a cot. The most important feature to look for when choosing a cot is the safety aspect. The sides should be securely held in place by childproof latches. The bars should be close enough together that baby can't get stuck between them. The mattress should be firm and fit well into the base of the cot so that a little head and fingers can't be trapped beneath. Some bed time extras you will need are: a plastic mattress protector; a fitted bottom sheet; mosquito net; cot bumper and a colourful mobile or toy to suspend over the cot.

☐ Change table
Any firm horizontal surface can become a very useful change table. Cover the surface, such as a table top, old desk or chest of drawers with some washable or spongeable covering. For very small babies a shaped foam pad with raised sides acts as a secure cradle when changing or dressing baby. Ideally the change table will have some drawers for holding all those change time essentials, such as creams, powder, pins, tissues, wash cloth and even a favourite toy to distract and amuse.

☐ Storage
You will be amazed at how much stuff such a little person needs. Plan for storage of various kinds to be nearest the place where the items will be used. Open shelves above the change table are ideal for stacking clean nappies, while drawers and cupboards are best for clothes. Some form of toy storage, stackable plastic cubes, shelves or a basket, will also be useful.

☐ Chair
There should be a comfortable chair, preferably with arm rests in some quiet corner for feeding baby or simply a moment's rest.

☐ Nappy Bucket
A simple plastic covered bucket will do very well for soaking soiled nappies. If you plan to use single-use nappies they can be disposed of in the bucket.

☐ Bath
Like the bassinet, small plastic babies' baths are best for the newborn. You will know when it's time to transfer to the family bath tub. Make sure that you have all of baby's bath time needs at hand before you begin.

☐ Night light
It is certain that you will be making many middle-of-the-night visits to the nursery. A night light, or dimmer switch on the main light, will allow you to move around comfortably without a bright light disturbing the baby.

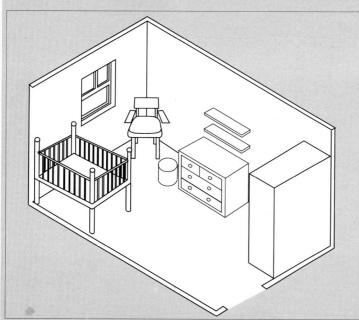

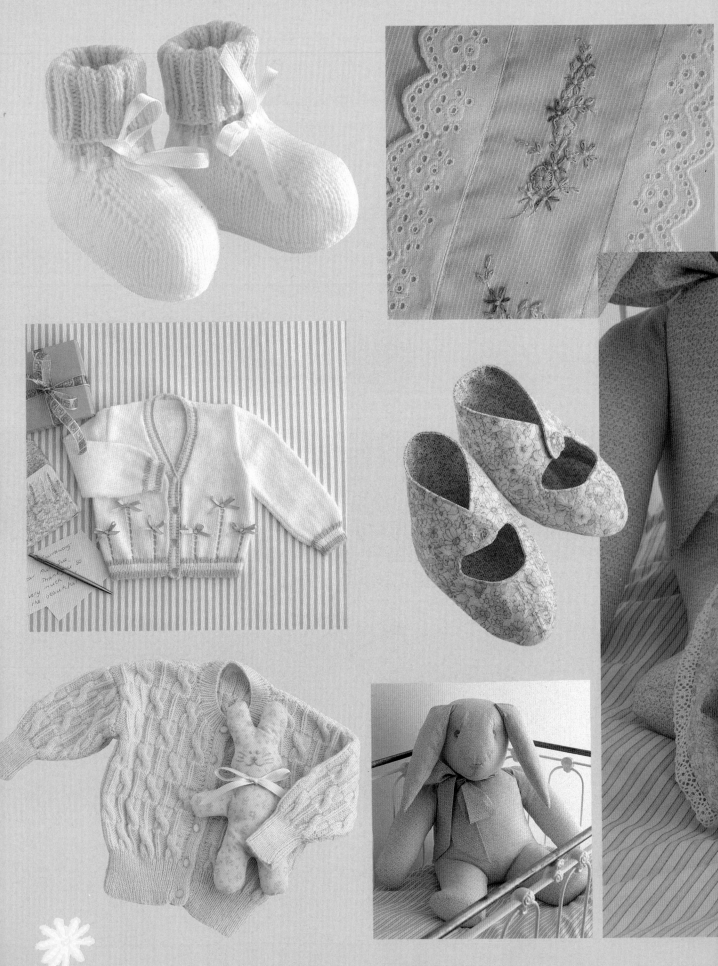

Blossom ✻

The promise of
beautiful things to
come – babies and
blossoms just seem to
go together. Even the
huge, cuddly bunny
is decked out in the
prettiest floral print.
If you've always
wanted to try
smocking, this little
dress is the perfect
way to begin.
Remember to make
the shoes and pants to
complete the picture
and top it all off with
a warm, textured
cardigan.

SMOCKED DRESS
AND PANTS

SIZE: 6 to 12 months

MATERIALS

- [ ] 1.10 m of 115 cm wide fabric
- [ ] three small buttons
- [ ] 1.2 m cotton lace
- [ ] embroidery thread for smocking

PATTERN
Pattern outline

13 front yoke (cut 2); 14 front skirt (cut 1);15 back yoke (cut 2); 16 back skirt (cut 2); 17 sleeves (cut 2); 18 front/back pants (cut 2)

Use same pattern as for yellow spotted dress and pants on page 22 omitting neck, hem and yoke frills. 1 cm seams allowed. Join all pieces together with right sides facing.

1 Smock dress front following instructions opposite. Pull up smocking to width of front yoke.
2 Sew front yoke to back yokes at shoulders with right sides facing. Press seams open. Sew front yoke facing to back yoke facings (extensions of back yoke), with right sides together. Press seams open.
3 Fold yoke facings over yokes so that right sides are facing. Stitch around neck edge. Trim seam, clip curve. Turn facing

to right side. Press.
4 Pin front yoke to front skirt with right sides together. Stitch, taking care to leave front yoke facing free.
5 Stitch centre back skirt seam up to opening. Finish skirt back opening edges as desired.
6 Pin back yokes to back skirt as far as foldline on back yokes. Fold back extensions to inside along foldlines, forming facings. Stitch through all thicknesses, taking care to leave back yoke facing free.
7 Press all seams towards yoke. Turn under seam allowance on raw lower edges of yokes.
8 Tack together raw armhole edges of yokes and from here on treat as a single layer. Gather sleeve heads. Sew sleeves into armholes, adjusting gathering to fit. Neaten armhole edges with overlock or zigzag stitching.
9 Turn under 4 cm at sleeve ends. Stitch raw edge down with two rows of stitching to form casings. Join ends of lace and stitch around sleeve ends, just under the edge as shown. Thread elastic through casings, adjust length and secure ends.
10 Sew side seams from wrist to hem.
11 Turn up hem. Press. Join ends of lace together. Tack lace around hem, just under the edge as shown. Stitch, fixing hem and lace as you go.
12 Make buttonholes in back yoke. Sew on buttons.
13 To make pants, sew inside leg seams.

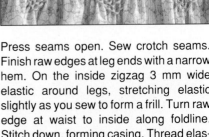

Press seams open. Sew crotch seams. Finish raw edges at leg ends with a narrow hem. On the inside zigzag 3 mm wide elastic around legs, stretching elastic slightly as you sew to form a frill. Turn raw edge at waist to inside along foldline. Stitch down, forming casing. Thread elastic through casing and secure ends.

♡ HINT ♡

For a truly professional finish it is important to press all your seams and stitching as you go. This is particularly so for seams which must be pressed open before the piece is sewn to another piece. Take care to adjust the temperature of your iron to the type of fabric you are working with.

SIMPLE SMOCKING

Smocking began as the first 'elastic' but has become a delightful and creative technique for trimming babies' and children's clothes.

Follow these illustrated steps to master the technique and some of the most common smocking stitches.

STEP 1 Mark dots on wrong side of fabric with a purchased smocking dot transfer or by tracing them off graph paper with clear points. You can also place carbon paper under the fabric, and pinning graph paper on top, firmly press out dots.

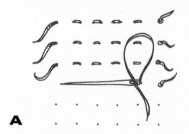

A

STEP 2 Gathering up dots: Using strong, doubled thread in a contrasting colour, begin at right hand side and pick up each dot across fabric. Leave threads hanging at ends. (Fig. A).

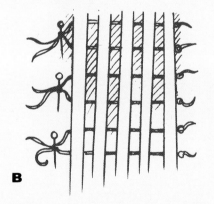

B

STEP 3 Pulling up: Pull up threads to desired width, for example width of yoke. (Fig. B). Tie off threads firmly in pairs. Pull up firmly, but not tightly. Secure threads. Begin smocking on right hand side. Remove gathering threads when smocking is complete.

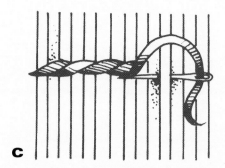

C

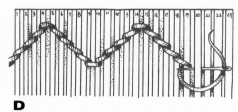

D

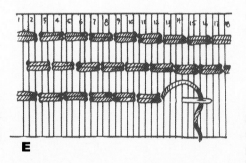

E

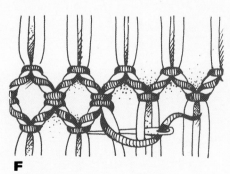

F

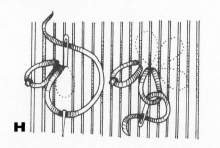

H

OUTLINE STITCH (Fig. C): Work stitch with thread above needle as shown and keeping stitches tight.

WAVE STITCH (Fig. D): Work stitches firmly although angles make this stitch very elastic. Always work between two rows of gathering stitches, beginning at lower left corner and working up as shown. When ascending, thread lies under needle and below when descending.

HONEYCOMBING (Fig. E): One of the oldest smocking stitches, it is very elastic and simple to do. Stagger starting points of stitches, working over two folds.

SURFACE HONEYCOMB (Fig. F): This stitch is elastic and very decorative, exposing more thread. It can be built up into panels by mirror reversing the panels.

BULLION KNOTS (Fig. G) and **LAZY DAISY STITCH** (Fig. H): These are worked as if embroidering but take care to begin and end stitches on folds as shown.

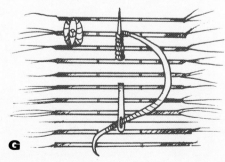

G

SHOES

SIZE: 6 to 12 months

MATERIALS
☐ 50 cm x 20 cm each of dress and contrasting fabric for lining
☐ 50 cm x 20 cm fusible interfacing
☐ two small buttons

PATTERN
1 upper (cut 2 main fabric, 2 contrast fabric, 2 interfacing); 2 sole (cut 2 main fabric, 2 contrast fabric, 2 interfacing). Cut out pattern pieces as directed. 6 mm seams allowed. Join all pieces with right sides facing.

1   Interface main fabric pieces. Join centre front seam. Press open. On outside, topstitch both sides of seam.
2   Join sole to shoe around circle through B and C. Press open and topstitch as before. Repeat for lining.
3   With right sides together, stitch lining to shoe all around edge, leaving an opening for turning and accessibility at centre back. Trim seam and clip curves. Turn and press. Close opening by hand. Edgestitch all around.
4   Make buttonholes. Sew on buttons.

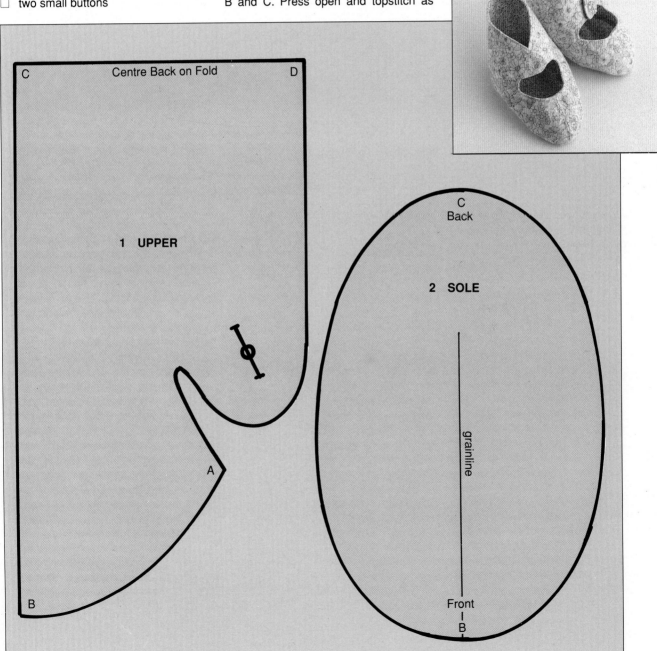

56

CARDIGAN WITH BOWS

BACK
Using 2.25 mm needles and C, cast on 75(83,91,99) sts.
1st row: K2, * P1, K1, rep from * to last st, K1.
2nd row: K1, * P1, K1, rep from * to end.
Rep 1st and 2nd rows once.
5th row: Using MC, knit.
6th row: As 2nd row.
Rep 1st and 2nd rows twice.
Using C, rep 5th and 6th rows once.
Rep 1st and 2nd rows once.
Change to 3 mm needles and MC .**
Work in st st (1 row K, 1 row P) until work measures 13(15,18,21) cm from beg, ending with a purl row.
Shape armholes
Cast off 5(5,6,6) sts at beg of next 2 rows.
Dec one st at each end of alt rows until 57(63,69,75) sts rem.
Work 33(35,39,41) rows.
Shape shoulders
Cast off 8(9,10,11) sts at beg of next 2 rows, then 8(10,11,12) sts at beg of foll 2 rows.
Cast off rem 25(25,27,29) sts.

LEFT FRONT
Using 2.25 mm needles and C, cast on 37(41,45,49) sts.
Work as given for Back to **.
1st row: K6(7,8,9), [yfwd, K2tog, K9(10,11,12)] twice, yfwd, K2tog, K7(8,9,10).
2nd row: Purl.
Rep last 2 rows 6(8,12,14) times more, then 1st and 2nd rows once.
Next row: K17(19,21,23), yfwd, K2tog, K18(20,22,24).
Next row: Purl.
Rep last 2 rows 4(6,6,8) times more.
Cont in st st until work measures same as Back to underarm, ending with a purl row.
Shape armhole and front slope
Cast off 5(5,6,6) sts at beg of next row.
Dec one st at armhole edge in alt rows 4(5,5,6) times, AT SAME TIME dec one st at front edge in alt rows 5(3,3,3) times, then in foll 4th rows until 16(19,21,23) sts rem.
Work 3 rows.

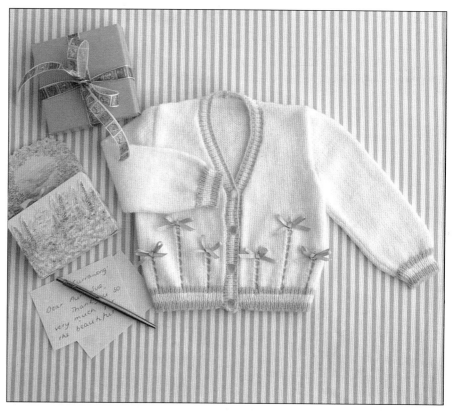

MEASUREMENTS

To fit underarm					
	cm	41	46	51	56
	ins	16	18	20	22
Actual measurement					
	cm	46	51	56	61
Length to back neck					
	cm	23	26	30	34
Sleeve seam	cm	14	17	20	24

MATERIALS
Cleckheaton Babysoft 3 ply (25 g) balls (or other suitable 3 ply): 4(4,5,5) balls Main Colour (MC); 1 ball Contrast (C); 1 pair each 3 mm (No. 11) and 2.25 mm (No. 13) knitting needles or the required size to give correct tension; 4(4,5,5) small buttons; ribbon.

TENSION
This garment has been designed at a tension of 32 sts to 10 cm over st st, using 3 mm needles.
It is important to knit a tension square and to work to the stated tension in order to obtain the required measurements. If your square is bigger use finer needles. If your square is smaller use thicker needles.

Shape shoulder
Cast off 8(9,10,11) sts at beg of next row.
Work 1 row.
Cast off.

RIGHT FRONT
Work Right Front to correspond with Left Front, reversing shapings and working one row more before shaping armhole and shoulder.

SLEEVES
Using 2.25 mm needles and C, cast on 41(43,45,45) sts.
Work 14 rows in rib and stripes as given for Back inc 8 sts evenly across last row. 49(51,53,53) sts.
Change to 3 mm needles and MC.
Cont in st st inc one st at each end of 5th and foll 8th(10th,10th,12th) row/s until there are 57(55,59,63) sts, **2nd, 3rd and 4th sizes only** — then in foll (12th,12th,14th) row/s until there are (59,63,65) sts.
Cont without shaping until side edge measures 14(17,20,24) cm from beg, ending with a purl row.
Shape top
Cast of 2(2,3,3) sts at beg of next 2 rows.
Dec one st at each end of next and foll alt rows until 33(33,29,29) sts rem, then in every row until 11 sts rem.
Cast off.

RIGHT FRONT BAND

Using back stitch, join shoulder seams. With right side facing, using 2.25 mm needles and C, knit up 109(121,139,157) sts evenly along right front edge to centre of back neck.

1st row: K1, * P1, K1, rep from * to end

2nd row: Using MC, knit.

3rd row: As 1st row.

4th row: Rib 4, [yfwd, K2tog, rib 15(17,15,17)] 3(3,4,4) times, yfwd, K2tog, rib to end.

4(4,5,5) buttonholes.

5th row: As 1st row.

6th row: Using C, as 2nd row.

7th row: As 1st row.

Cast off loosely in rib.

LEFT FRONT BAND

Using 2.25 mm needles and C, beg at centre of back neck, knit up 109(121,139,157) sts evenly along half of back neck and along left front edge. Complete as given for Right Front Band omitting buttonholes.

TO MAKE UP

Press lightly on wrong side with cool iron. Using back stitch, join side and sleeve seams, sew bands together at centre back neck. Sew in sleeves. Sew on buttons. Thread ribbon through eyelet holes on Fronts. Make 6 small bows and attach to top of ribbon on each Front as illustrated. Sew on buttons.

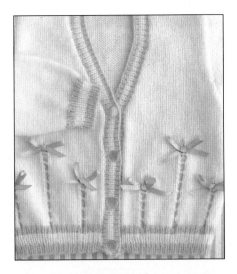

CABLE CARDIGAN

BACK

Using 2.25 mm needles, cast on 75(83,91,99) sts.

1st row: K2, * P1, K1, rep from * to last st, K1.

2nd row: K1, * P1, K1, rep from * to end.

Rep 1st and 2nd rows 12 times more, inc 12(14,16,16) sts evenly across last row. 87(97,107,115) sts.

Change to 3 mm needles.

1st row: P1(6,0,1), K1(1,0,1), P3(3,1,3), * K6, P4, K1, P3, rep from * to last 12(17,8,12) sts, K6, P4(4,2,4), K1(1,0,1), P1(6,0,1).

2nd and alt rows: Knit all knit sts and purl all purl sts as they appear.

Rep 1st and 2nd rows twice more.

7th row: P1(6,0,1), K1(1,0,1), P3(3,1,3), * C6F, P4, K1, P3, rep from * to last 12(17,8,12) sts, C6F, P4(4,2,4), K1(1,0,1), P1(6,0,1).

8th row: As 2nd row.

Rep 1st and 2nd rows twice more.

13th row: P8(3,4,8), K1(0,1,1), P3(0,3,3), * K6, P4, K1, P3, rep from * to last 5(10,1,5) st/s, K0(6,0,0), P5(4,1,5).

14th row: As 2nd row.

Rep 13th and 14th rows twice more.

19th row: P8(3,4,8), K1(0,1,1), P3(0,3,3), * C6F, P4, K1, P3, rep from * to last 5(10,1,5) sts/s, (C6F) 0(1,0,0) time/s, P5(4,1,5).

MEASUREMENTS

To fit underarm	cm	41	46	51	56
	ins	16	18	20	22
Actual measurement					
	cm	45	50	55	60
Length to back neck					
	cm	23	26	30	34
Sleeve seam	cm	13	15	18	21

MATERIALS

Cleckheaton Babysoft 3 Ply (25 g) balls (or other suitable 3 ply): 3 (4,4,5); 1 pair each 3 mm (No. 11) and 2.25 (No. 13) knitting needles or the required size to give correct tension; 2 stitch holders; 6(6,6,7) buttons; a cable needle.

ABBREVIATIONS

C6F = Slip next 3 sts onto cable needle and leave at front of work, K3, then K3 from cable needle.

TENSION

This garment has been designed at a tension of 38 sts to 10 cm over patt, using 3 mm needles and 32 sts to 10 cm over st st, using 3 mm needles.
It is important to knit a tension square and to work to the stated tension in order to obtain the required measurements. If your square is bigger use finer needles. If your square is smaller use thicker needles.

20th row: As 2nd row.

Rep 13th and 14th rows twice more.

Last 24 rows form patt.

Cont in patt until work measures 22.5(25.5,29.5,33.5) cm from beg, working last row on wrong side.

Shape shoulders

Keeping patt correct, cast off 10(11,13,14) sts at beg of next 4 rows, then 10(12,12,13) sts at beg of foll 2 rows.

Leave rem 27(29,31,33) sts on a stitch holder.

LEFT FRONT

Using 2.25 mm needles, cast on 37(41,45,49) sts.

Work 26 rows in rib as given for lower band of Back, inc 6(7,8,8) sts evenly across last row. 43(48,53,57) sts.

Change to 3 mm needles. **

1st row: P1(6,0,1), K1(1,0,1), P3(3,1,3), (K6, P4, K1, P3) 2(2,3,3) times, K6, P4.

2nd and alt rows: Knit all knit sts and purl all purl sts as they appear.

Rep 1st and 2nd rows twice more.

7th row: P1(6,0,1), K1(1,0,1), P3(3,1,3), (C6F, P4, K1, P3) 2(2,3,3) times, C6F, P4.

8th row: As 2nd row.

Rep 1st and 2nd rows twice more.

13th row: P8(3,4,8), K1(0,1,1), P3(0,3,3,), (K6, P4, K1, P3) 2(3,3,3) times, P3.

14th row: As 2nd row.

Rep 13th and 14th rows twice more.

19th row: P8(3,4,8), K1(0,1,1), P3(0,3,3), (C6F, P4, K1, P3) 2(3,3,3) times, P3.

20th row: As 2nd row.

Rep 13th and 14th rows twice more.

Last 24 rows form patt.

Cont in patt until there are 17(19,21,23) rows less than Back to Shoulder shaping.

Shape neck

Next row (wrong side facing): Cast off

7(8,9,10) sts, patt to end.
Work 1 row.
Keeping patt correct, dec one st at neck edge in foll alt rows 6 times. 30(34,38,41) sts.
Work 3(5,7,9) rows in patt.

Shape shoulder
Cast off 10(11,13,14) sts at beg of next row and foll alt row.
Work 1 row. Cast off.

RIGHT FRONT
Work as for Left Front to **.
1st row: P3, (K6, P4, K1, P3) 2(2,3,3) times, K6, P4(4,2,4), K1(1,0,1), P1(6,0,1).
2nd and alt rows: Knit all knit sts and purl all purl sts as they appear.
Rep 1st and 2nd rows twice more.
7th row: P3, (C6F, P4, K1, P3) 2(2,3,3) times, C6F, P4(4,2,4), K1(1,0,1), P1(6,0,1).
8th row: As 2nd row.
Rep 1st and 2nd rows twice more.
13th row: P6, K1, P3, (K6, P4, K1, P3) 2(2,3,3) times, K0(6,0,0), P5(4,1,5).
14th row: As 2nd row.
Rep 13th and 14th rows twice more.
19th row: P6, K1, P3, (C6F, P4, K1, P3) 2(2,3,3) times, (C6F) 0(1,0,0) time/s, P5(4,1,5).
20th row: As 2nd row.
Rep 13th and 14th rows twice more.
Last 24 rows form patt.
Cont in patt until there are 16(18,20,22) rows less than Back to shoulder shaping.

Shape neck
Next row (right side facing): Cast off 7(8,9,10) sts, patt to end.
Keeping patt correct, dec one st at neck edge in foll alt rows 6 times. 30(34,38,41) sts.
Work 4(6,8,10) rows in patt.

Shape shoulder
Complete as for Left Front.

SLEEVES
Using 2.25 mm needles, cast on 43(47,49,49) sts.
Work 26 rows in rib as given for lower band of Back, inc 10 sts evenly across last row. 53(57,59,59) sts.
Change to 3 mm needles.
1st row: Inc in first st, P1(3,4,4), (K6, P4, K1, P3) 3 times, K6, P2(4,5,5), inc in last st.
2nd and alt rows: Knit all knit sts and purl all purl sts as they appear.
Keeping patt correct (as given for Back), work 10 rows, at same time inc one st at each end of next and foll alt rows 5 times. 65(69,71,71) sts.

13th row: Inc in first st, P0(2,3,3), (K6, P4, K1, P3) 4 times, K6, P1(3,4,4), inc in last st. 67(71,73,73) sts.
Keeping patt correct, inc one st at each end of foll alt rows twice, then in foll 4th rows 1(2,5,8) time/s, noting to work extra sts made into patt whenever possible. 73(79,87,93) sts.
Cont in patt, without shaping, until side edge measures 13(15,18,21) cm from beg, working last row on wrong side.

Shape top
Cast off 6(6,7,8) sts at beg of next 6 rows.
Cast off rem sts loosely.

LEFT FRONT BAND
Using 2.25 mm needles, cast on 9 sts.
1st row: K2, (P1, K1) 3 times, K1.
2nd row: K1, (P1, K1) 4 times. ***
Rep 1st and 2nd rows 39(44,54,59) times.
Break off yarn, leave sts on stitch holder.

RIGHT FRONT BAND
Work as for Left Front Band to ***.
Rep 1st and 2nd rows once.
**** **5th row:** Rib 4, cast off 2 sts, rib 3.
6th row: Rib 3, cast on 2 sts, rib 4.
Work 14(16,20,18) rows rib. ****

Rep from **** to **** 3(3,3,4) times, then 5th and 6th rows once.
5(5,5,6) buttonholes.
Work 11(13,17,15) rows rib.
DO NOT BREAK OFF YARN, leave sts on needle.

NECKBAND
Using back stitch, join shoulder seams.
With right side facing, using 2.25 mm needles, holding right front band sts, knit up 73(81,89,97) sts evenly around neck edge, including sts from back neck stitch holder, then rib across left front band sts. 91(99,107,115) sts.
Work 9 rows rib as for lower band of Back, beg with a 2nd row and working a buttonhole (as before) in 4th and 5th rows.
Cast off loosely in rib.

TO MAKE UP
Do not press. Using back stitch, sew in sleeves, placing centre of sleeves to shoulder seams, then sew up side and sleeve seams. Sew front bands in position. Sew on buttons.

BOOTEES WITH RIB ANKLE

Using 3 mm needles and MC, cast on 43 sts.
Work as for Lemon Scented Bootees on page 78 to ***.
Work 10 rows st st (1 row K, 1 row P).

Shape instep
Next row: K37 K2tog, turn.
Next row: Sl1, P9, P2tog, turn.
Next row: Sl1, K9, K2tog, turn.
Rep last 2 rows until 45 sts rem (17 sts on each side of instep).
Next row: Sl1, K9, K2tog, K16.
Next row: Purl. 44 sts.

Ankle
Next row: K1, * yfwd, K2tog, rep from * to last st, K1.
Next row: Using C, purl, inc one st at each end. 46 sts.
Next row: K2, * P2, K2, rep from * to end.
Next row: P2, *K2, P2, rep from * to end.

MEASUREMENTS
To fit 0-6 months
NOTE: For slightly smaller bootees, use one size smaller needles than those which give correct tension. For slightly larger bootees, use one size larger needles than those which give correct tension.

MATERIALS
Cleckheaton Babysoft 3 Ply (25 g) balls (or other suitable 3 ply): 1 ball each Main Colour (MC) and Contrast (C); 1 pair 3 mm (No. 11) knitting needles or the required size to give correct tension; about 85 cm of 6 mm wide ribbon.

TENSION
32 sts to to cm over st st, using 3 mm needles
It is important to knit a tension square and to work to the stated tension in order to obtain the required measurements. If your square is bigger use finer needles. If your square is smaller use thicker needles.

Rep last 2 rows until rib section measures 8 cm from beg, working last row on wrong side.
Cast off.

TO MAKE UP
Using a flat seam, join foot and back seam, reversing back seam for 4 cm at ankle edge. Thread ribbon through eyelet holes and tie in a bow. Fold half rib section onto right side.

GIANT PINK BUNNY

MATERIALS
☐ 1.5 m of 115 cm wide cotton fabric
☐ polyester fibre for stuffing
☐ embroidery thread and scraps of felt for face

PATTERN
Pattern outline ——————— grey
23 front body (cut 2); 24 back lower body and legs (cut 1); 25 upper back (cut 2); 26 side head (cut 2); 27 head gusset (cut 1); 28 ears (cut 4); 29 arms (cut 4); 30 soles (cut 2)
Cut out pattern pieces as directed.
1 cm seams allowed. Clip all curved seam allowances.

1   Sew darts in head. Join head sections together from nose to large darts at neck.

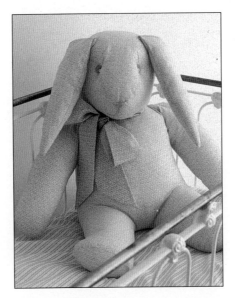

Insert head gusset into head, matching nose. Stuff head. Place ear sections together with right sides facing. Stitch, leaving straight edge open. Turn and press. Stuff lightly. Turn under 6 mm on raw edge and open out into oval shape. Sew ears to head at top darts.

2   Join fronts together at centre front. Sew upper leg sections to lower edges of front body. Place front and lower back body together with right sides facing. Stitch inside leg seams in one continuous seam, reinforcing stitching and clipping carefully into corners.
3   Sew upper back sections to lower back from dart to edges of legs. Make dart and continue stitching, joining centre back seam.
4   Attach one arm section at each marking on front and back body. With right sides together, stitch continuously from outside foot up sides of body and around arms, leaving open at neck edges for stuffing. Sew soles to feet. Turn and stuff.
5   Place head on body, adjust to a pleasing angle and handsew into place.
6   Embroider nose with satin stitch, mouth with chain stitch as shown. Contour eye sockets by stitching across from one eye to the other with thread doubled for extra strength, through head, and pulling thread slightly. Blanket stitch small white felt circles into place for eyes and black circles for pupils.

PILGRIM BONNET

SIZE: 12 months

MATERIALS
- ☐ 80 cm of 115 cm wide cotton
- ☐ 1 m of bias binding
- ☐ 1.5 m of 1 cm wide ribbon
- ☐ fusible interfacing
- ☐ 1 m of cotton lace

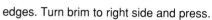

PATTERN
1 cm seams allowed. Clip all curves. Join all pieces with right sides facing.

Cut out pattern pieces as directed. Cut two straps each 7 cm x 40 cm.

NOTE: The measurement A to B is the number of cm from 3 cm below one ear, over top of head to just below other ear, plus 3 cm; X to Y is number of cm from front hairline to nape of neck (approx 30 cm); C to D is twice measurement A to B.

1   Mark crown centre points X and Y. At X, 4 cm from edge, iron a small piece of interfacing to wrong side of fabric. Make two small buttonholes as marked.

2   Sew bias binding around curved edge of crown, on wrong side of fabric, 4 cm from edge to form casing. Thread two lengths of ribbon through casing, securing one edge of each at straight edge of crown, and having the other end emerge through a buttonhole.

3   Press under narrow hem around curved edge. Stitch lace under this edge, fixing hem in place as you go.

4   Gather straight edge of crown between casing.

5   Interface brim. Fold brim over double with right sides together and stitch short ends. Turn in seam allowance on raw edges. Turn brim to right side and press.

6   Draw up gathering on crown, having most of the gathering towards the centre. Insert gathered edge between pressed edges of brim, aligning brim edges with gathering stitches. Stitch close to pressed edge through all thicknesses.

7   Fold straps over double with right sides together. Stitch long side and one short end at an angle. Trim seams, turn and press. Stitch straps to both sides of bonnet at casing points, folding under and pleating raw edge of straps. Stitch over end of straps in shape of box.

8   Draw up ribbon to gather crown and tie in a bow.

EMBROIDERED SHEETS

MATERIALS
- ☐ 1.6 m of 115 cm wide sheer cotton
- ☐ 1.3 m cottonlace trim
- ☐ embroidery thread

1   Cut a length of fabric 10 cm x 115 cm. Draw outline of flowers directly onto fabric using a sharp pencil. Embroider flowers on centre of this panel using lazy daisy stitch, french knots, blanket stitch and back stitch. Enlarge flower design to the size you wish.

2   Stitch lace along both edges of right side of panel with raw edges even. Place panel on top edge of sheet with right side of panel facing wrong side of sheet. Stitch along top edge. Turn panel to right side. Turn under raw edge of fabric under lace and stitch down just inside edge of fabric. Topstitch top edge to match. Press.

3   Neaten and hem all raw edges of sheet.

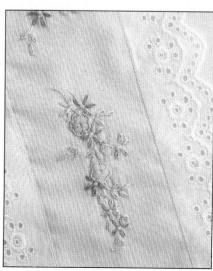

Nursery Pets

A teddy or two and a bunny to cuddle – fill your baby's world with these loveable friends. They can be knitted or sewn, cuddled or worn, slept on and so much more! We've chosen primary brights for our pet parade but you might prefer pastels or even black and white for a super-sophisticated look.

TEDDY BEAR
SAMPLER

Work this sampler on Aida 14 cloth, using two strands of DMC and following this stitch and colour guide.

CROSS STITCH

■	DMC	310	Black
/	DMC	796	Blue
◢	DMC	797	Blue
✕	DMC	799	Blue
⌒	DMC	800	Blue
—	DMC	972	Yellow
Λ	DMC	986	Green
•	DMC	987	Green
⊤	DMC	989	Green
‡	DMC	433	Brown
⟩	DMC	434	Brown
○	DMC	436	Brown
✓	DMC	437	Brown
△	DMC	304	Red
⟍	DMC	666	Red

BACKSTITCH

DMC	310	Around ribbon
DMC	304	Lettering
DMC	3031	Bear

RUNNING STITCH

DMC	799	Inside border edge

BABY'S OVERALL AND JUMPER

JUMPER

BACK

Using 3 mm needles and C1, cast on 69(75,81) sts.

1st row: K2, * P1, K1, rep from * to last st, K1.

2nd row: K1, * P1, K1, rep from * to end.

Rep 1st and 2nd rows 5(6,7) times more.
Change to 3.75 mm needles and MC.
Cont in st st (1 row K, 1 row P) until work measures 11.5(11.5,14) cm from beg, ending with a purl row.

Proceed in patt as follows:

1st and 2nd rows: Using C1, knit.

NOTE: When changing colours in centre of row, twist the colour to be used underneath and to the right of colour just used, making sure both yarns are worked firmly at joins. Always change colours on wrong side of work so colour change does not show on right side. Use a separate ball of yarn for each section of colour. We suggest using bobbins. Wind a quantity of yarn around bobbin and place end through slot to hold. Unwind only enough yarn to knit required sts, then place yarn in slot, keeping bobbin close to work.

Work rows 3 to 18 inclusive from Graph A.

19th and 20th rows: Using C1, knit.

Using MC, work 2 rows in st st.

Shape armholes

Cast off 4 sts at beg of next 2 rows.
Dec one st at each end of every row 5 times. 51(57,63) sts. **
Work 1 row.

Divide for back opening

1st row: K28(31,34), turn.

2nd row: K5, purl to end.

Rep last 2 rows 2(3,3) times more.

Next row: Knit to last 3 sts, yfwd, K2tog (buttonhole), K1.

Keeping garter st border correct, work 11(11,9) rows, then work buttonhole row once. **3rd size only** — rep last 10 rows once more.

All sizes — 2(2,3) buttonholes.

Keeping garter st border correct, work 7(7,5) rows.

Shape shoulder

Next row: Cast off 7(9,10) sts, knit to end.

MEASUREMENTS

To fit underarm	cm	46	51	56
	ins	18	20	22
Jumper				
Actual measurement				
	cm	51	56	61
Length to back neck				
	cm	27	28	32
Sleeve seam	cm	15	17.5	20.5
Overall				
Inside leg length (excluding cuff)				
	cm	18	20	22
Outside leg length to beg rib waist (excluding cuff)				
	cm	38	41	44

MATERIALS

Cleckheaton 5 Ply Machine Wash (50 g) balls (or other suitable 5 ply): 2 balls Main Colour (MC — Blue), 1 ball each 1st Contrast (C1 — Red), 2nd Contrast (C2 — White) for Jumper; 4(4,5) balls MC; 1 ball each C1, C2 for Overall; 1 pair each 3.75 mm (No. 9) and 3 mm (No. 11) knitting needles or the required size to give correct tension; 3 stitch holders, 3(3,4) buttons, bobbins for Jumper; 1 stitch holder, 4 buttons, bobbins, length of round elastic (if desired) for Overall.

TENSION

These garments have been designed at a tension of 26 sts to 10 cm over st st, using 3.75 mm needles.

It is important to knit a tension square and to work to the stated tension in order to obtain the required measurements. If your square is bigger use finer needles. If your square is smaller use thicker needles.

Next row: K5, purl to end.

Next row: Cast off 8(9,10) sts, knit to end. Break off yarn and leave rem 13(13,14) sts on stitch holder.

With right side facing, join MC to rem sts, cast on 5 sts (for underlap) and complete to correspond with other side, omitting buttonholes.

FRONT

Work as for Back to **.

Work 13(13,17) rows in st st.

Shape neck

Next row: Using MC, K19(22,25), turn.

Dec one st at neck edge in foll alt rows 4(4,5) times. 15(18,20) sts.
Work 5(7,7) rows in st st.

Shape shoulder

Cast off 7(9,10) sts at beg of next row.
Work 1 row.
Cast off.

Slip next 13 sts onto a stitch holder and leave. Join MC to rem sts and complete to correspond with other side.

SLEEVES

Using 3 mm needles and C1, cast on 39(41,41) sts.

Work 10(12,14) rows in rib as given for lower band of Back, inc 2(4,6) sts evenly across last row. 41(45,47) sts.
Change to 3.75 mm needles.

1st row: Using C1, inc in first st, knit to last st, inc in last st.

2nd row: Knit.

Work rows 3 to 18 inclusive from Graph B, AT SAME TIME, inc one st at each end of 7th(5th,3rd) row, then in foll 8th(6th,4th) row, **3rd size only** — then in foll 6th row. 47(51,55) sts.

Using C1, knit 2 rows in garter st.

Using MC and working in st st, inc one st at each end of 5th(next,next) row then in foll 8th(8th,6th) row/s 1(2,4) time/s. 51(57,65) sts.

Cont without shaping until side edge measures 15(17.5,20.5) cm from beg, ending with a purl row.

Shape top

Cast off 2 sts at beg of next 2 rows.

Dec one st at each end of next and foll alt rows 8(7,8) times in all, then in every row until 13(13,15) sts rem.

Cast off.

NECKBAND

Using back stitch, join shoulder seams.
With right side facing, using 3 mm needles and C1, beg at left back opening, knit

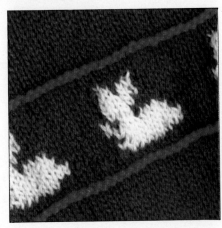

across 13(13,14) sts on left back neck stitch holder, knit up 13(15,17) sts evenly along left side of neck, knit across 13 sts from front stitch holder, knit up 13(15,17) sts evenly along right side of neck, knit across 13(13,14) sts on right back neck stitch holder. 65(69,75) sts.

1st row: K5, * P1, K1, rep from * to last 6 sts, P1, K5.

2nd row: K5, rib to last 5 sts, K2, yfwd, K2tog (buttonhole), K1.

Keeping garter st borders correct, work 3 rows in rib.

Cast off loosely in rib.

TO MAKE UP

Using back stitch, join side and sleeve seams, then sew in sleeves. Sew on buttons.

PANTS

RIGHT LEG (beg at waist)

Using 3 mm needles and MC, cast on 91(101,109) sts loosely.

Work 8(10,10) rows rib as for lower band of Back of Jumper.

Change to 3.75 mm needles.

Work 2 rows st st (1 row K, 1 row P).

NOTE: When turning, bring yarn to front of work, slip next st onto right hand needle, ybk, slip st back onto left hand needle, then turn and proceed as instructed. This avoids holes in work.

1st row: K16, turn.

2nd and alt rows: Purl.

3rd row: K22, turn.

5th row: K28, turn.

Cont turning in this manner, working 6 more sts in every knit row until the row "K52(58,64), turn" has been worked.

Next row: As 2nd row.

Cont until short side measures 20(21,22) cm from beg, ending with a purl row.

Shape crotch

Cast off 3 sts at beg of next 2 rows. 85(95,103) sts.

Cont in st st until work measures 6(11.5,20) cm from "shape crotch", ending with a purl row.

Using C1, knit 2 rows in garter st.

NOTE: When changing colours in centre of row, twist the colour to be used underneath and to the right of colour just used, making sure both yarns are worked firmly at joins. Always change colours on wrong side of work so colour change does not show on right side. Use a separate ball of yarn for each section of colour. We sug-

gest using bobbins. Wind a quantity of yarn around bobbin and place end through slot to hold. Unwind only enough yarn to knit required sts, then place yarn in slot, keeping bobbin close to work.

Work rows 3 to 18 inclusive from Graph C.

19th and 20th rows: Using C1, knit.

Using MC, work 2 rows in st st, dec 12(14,16) sts evenly across last row. 73(81,87) sts.

Change to 3 mm needles.

Work 28 rows in rib as for beg of Leg.

Cast off loosely in rib.

LEFT LEG

Work to correspond with Right Leg.

FRONT BODICE

Using back stitch, join centre front seam and centre back seam.

Using 3.75 mm needles and MC, cast on 39(43,49) sts loosely.

Work 4(6,8) rows st st.

Using C1, knit 2 rows in garter st.

Work rows 3 to 18 inclusive from Graph D.

Using C1, knit 2 rows in garter st.

Using MC, work 2(4,4) rows st st.

Leave sts on stitch holder.

SIDE STRIPS (Make 2)

Using 3 mm needles and C1, cast on 8 sts.

Cont in garter st (1st row on wrong side) until strip measures same as Front Bodice, working last row on wrong side.

Leave sts on spare needle.

TOP BORDER OF BODICE

Using 3 mm needles and C1, knit across first side strip, knit across sts on Front Bodice stitch holder, knit across 2nd side strip. 55(59,65) sts.

Knit 9 rows in garter st.

Cast off.

BACK BODICE

Using 3.75 mm needles and MC, cast on 39(43,49) sts loosely.

Work 40(50,58) rows in st st.

Leave sts on stitch holder.

SIDE STRIPS (Make 2)

Using 3 mm needles and C1, cast on 8 sts.

Cont in garter st (1st row is wrong side) until strip measures same as Back Bodice, working last row on wrong side.

Leave sts on spare needle.

TOP BORDER OF BODICE

Using 3 mm needles and C1, knit across 1st side strip, knit across sts on Back stitch holder, knit across 2nd side strip. 55(59,65) sts.

Knit 9 rows in garter st.

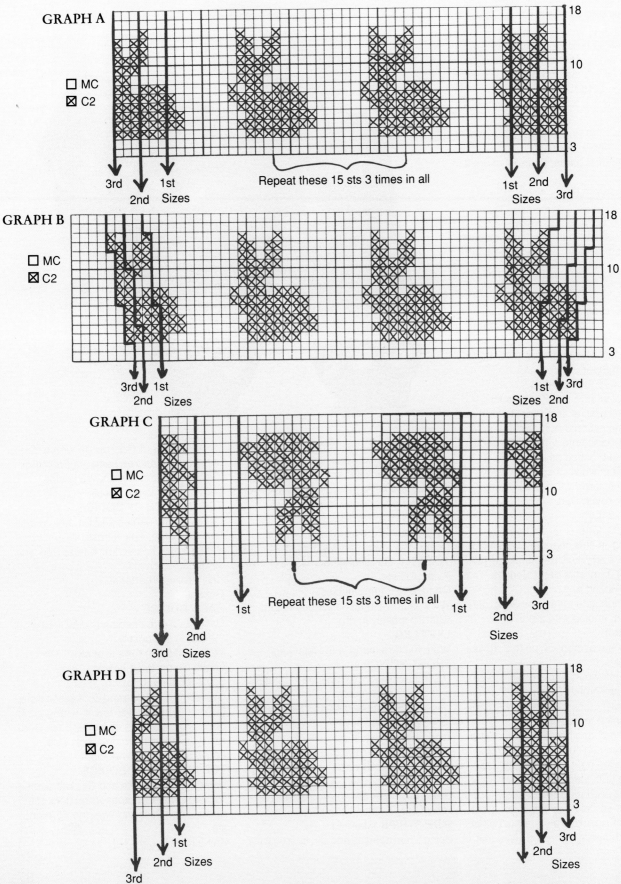

GRAPH A

☐ MC
☒ C2

Repeat these 15 sts 3 times in all

3rd
2nd
1st
Sizes

1st
Sizes
2nd
3rd

18
10
3

GRAPH B

☐ MC
☒ C2

3rd
2nd
1st
Sizes

1st
Sizes
2nd
3rd

18
10
3

GRAPH C

☐ MC
☒ C2

1st

Repeat these 15 sts 3 times in all

1st
2nd
Sizes
3rd

3rd
2nd
Sizes

18
10
3

GRAPH D

☐ MC
☒ C2

1st
2nd
Sizes
3rd

2nd
Sizes
3rd

18
10
3

Divide for shoulder straps.

Next row: K15(16,18), cast off 25(27,29), K15(16,18).

Cont on last 15(16,18) sts until shoulder strap measures 8(10,12) cm from dividing for straps, working last row on wrong side.

Next row: K3, K2tog, yfwd, K5(6,8), yfwd, K2tog, K3.

Knit 5 rows in garter st.

Cast off.

Join C1 to rem sts and complete as for other Shoulder Strap.

TO MAKE UP

Press lightly on wrong side, using a warm iron and damp cloth, if desired. Using back stitch, join leg seams, noting to reverse seam for 2.5 cm at lower edge for cuff. Sew Back and Front side strips to side edges of Bodices. Using back stitch, sew Back and Front Bodice to centre Back and Front of Overall (noting to sew st for st to rib of Overall, so that pants will slip over baby easily). Thread elastic through 3 rows of rib at waist (if desired). Narrow, flat elastic or round "hat" elastic is most suitable. Sew on buttons to Front Bodice to match buttonholes on Shoulder Straps.

SPOTTED SUNSUIT

SIZE: 0 to 6 months

NOTE: The suit is lined and appliqued in white pique. For applique pattern, see outline on page 32.

MATERIALS

- ☐ 40 cm of 115 cm wide spotted cotton
- ☐ 40 cm of 115 cm wide white pique
- ☐ scrap of white fabric for applique
- ☐ 11 hammer-on snaps
- ☐ 75 cm of 1 cm wide elastic
- ☐ small amount fusible interfacing

PATTERN

Pattern outline • • • • • • • • • • • • • • • • •

5 upper front (cut 4, two are for lining); 6 back and lower front (cut 2, one is for lining)

Cut out pattern pieces as directed. Trace, cut out and interface applique motif. 1 cm seams allowed. Join all pieces together with right sides facing.

1   Sew motif onto left front, using narrow zigzag stitches. Trim fabric close to stitching. Stitch again using wider satin stitch, covering raw edge and previous stitching.

2   Stitch shoulder seams of suit and of lining. Pin suit and lining together with right sides facing. Stitch, leaving waist edge of front open. Reinforce corners with double stitching. Trim seams, cut into corners and clip curves. Turn and press.

3   To form leg casings, run two rows of stitching around curved leg ends from A to B. Cut two 29 cm lengths of elastic and insert into casings through open waist edge. Secure ends.

4   To form waist casing, neaten raw edges together, and turn in 1.5 cm. Press casing to inside along foldline. Stitch. Thread 17 cm elastic through casing. Smooth out elastic at each end of casing and stitch through casing about 1.5 cm from each end. Pull out ends of elastic and trim excess. Stitch across ends of casing.

5   Overlap fronts with centres matching. Hammer on snaps, as shown on pattern. Attach front to back at sides with one hammer-on snap at large dot.

♡ HINT ♡

Hammer-on snaps are a convenient closure for babies' clothing. They are very easy to release in a great hurry and cope well with repeated washing. Always follow the manufacturer's instructions for applying them.

TEDDY BEAR QUILT

It looks complicated but is so simple! This quilt is made with a purchased cot quilt panel which is available at many craft and haberdashery stores. Tack the edges of the panel to a similar sized piece of polyester wadding. Embroider the motif outlines with handsewing. An embroidery hoop will make this much easier. Stitch along the vertical and horizontal lines of the panel as well, to give the effect of quilting. You can use matching or contrasting sewing thread, depending on the effect you want to create. Choose a complementary fabric for the quilt back, cut to the same size as the front. Bind the edges as for the patchwork quilt on page 7 and there you have it!

GIANT RED BUNNY

MATERIALS
☐ 1.5 m of 115 cm wide cotton fabric
☐ polyester fibre for stuffing
☐ embroidery thread and scraps of felt for face

PATTERN
Pattern outline ——————— grey
23 front body (cut 2); 24 back lower body and legs (cut 1); 25 upper back (cut 2); 26 side head (cut 2); 27 head gusset (cut 1); 28 ears (cut 4); 29 arms (cut 4); 30 soles (cut 2)
Cut out pattern pieces as directed. 1 cm seams allowed. Clip all curved seam allowances.

1   Sew darts in head. Join head sections together from nose to large darts at neck. Insert head gusset into head, matching nose. Stuff head. Place ear sections together with right sides facing. Stitch, leaving straight edge open. Turn and press. Stuff lightly. Turn under 6 mm on raw edge and open out into oval shape. Sew ears to

head at top darts.
2   Join fronts together at centre front. Sew upper leg sections to lower edges of front body. Place front and lower back body together with right sides facing. Stitch inside leg seams in one continuous seam, reinforcing stitching and clipping into corners.
3   Sew upper back sections to lower back from dart to edges of legs. Make dart and continue stitching centre back seam.

4   Attach one arm section at each marking on front and back body. With right sides together, stitch continuously from outside foot up sides of body and around arms, leaving open at neck edges for stuffing. Sew soles to feet. Turn and stuff.
5   Place head on body, adjust to a pleasing angle and handsew into place.
6   Embroider nose with satin stitch, mouth with chain stitch as shown. Contour eye sockets by stitching across from one eye to the other with thread doubled for extra strength, through head, and pulling thread slightly. Blanket stitch small white felt circles into place for eyes and black circles for pupils.

TOY SAFETY

When making toys for babies and small children it is essential to consider the safety aspect. We have used felt or embroidered eyes on all our toys for this reason. Make sure that any trims you use are sewn on very securely. Give them a good tug just to make sure they won't come off.

BABY BEARS

MATERIALS

- ☐ 20 cm of 115 cm wide cotton fabric
- ☐ polyester fibre for stuffing
- ☐ scraps of felt for eyes
- ☐ embroidery thread

PATTERN

Enlarge pattern pieces to actual size, and cut out as directed. Add 1 cm seam allowances all around. Join all pieces with right sides facing. Clip all curves.

1 Sew arms and legs, leaving upper straight edge open. Turn and stuff firmly.
2 Sew pairs of body sections together along curved edge. Sew two halves of body together, leaving neck edge open. Turn and stuff firmly.
3 Sew ears around curved edge. Turn. Turn in 6 mm along raw edge. Stuff lightly. Sew centre front and back head seams. Join front and back head. Turn and stuff firmly.
4 Using thread doubled, gather neck edge of body. Pull up and secure.
5 Sew arms, legs, head and ears to body.
6 Embroider eyes on using buttonhole stitch. Embroider nose in satin stitch and mouth in chain or stem stitch.

BABY BEAR GRID PATTERN

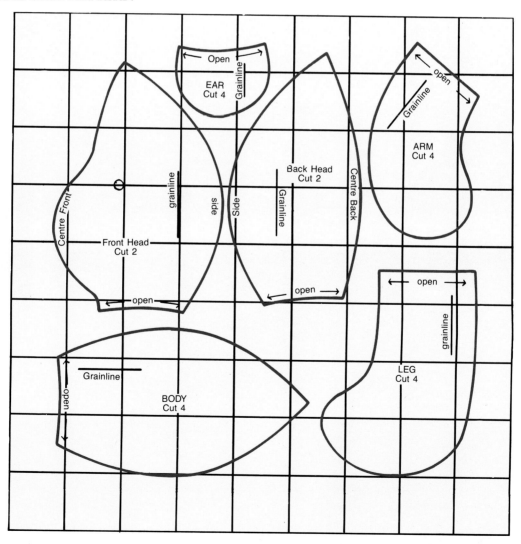

Each square is 2.5 cm x 2.5 cm

Lemon scented

Whether the stork delivers a baby boy or girl, you'll be safe with this collection of pretty lemon knits. Team some more lemon with the neatest pair of cuffed overalls you'll ever see. And you can gather it all up into the wonderful carry-all bag, which doubles as a changing pad.

FAIR ISLE JUMPER AND OVERALLS

JUMPER

BACK

Using 2.75 mm needles and C1, cast on 69(77,85) sts.

1st row: K2, * P1, K1, rep from * to last st, K1.

2nd row: K1, * P1, K1, rep from * to end.

Rep 1st and 2nd rows until band measures 3 cm from beg, ending with a 2nd row. Change to 3.25 mm needles.

1st row: Using MC, K1, * yfwd, K2tog, rep from * to end.

Work 3 rows st st (1 row K, 1 row P), beg with a purl row.

Change to 3.75 mm needles.

NOTE: Do not weave colours in Fair Isle patt, but carry colour not in use loosely across on wrong side. Always carry colours to end of row.

** **5th row:** K1C1, * K2MC, K2C1, rep from * to end.

6th row: P1MC, * P2C1, P2MC, rep from * to end.

7th row: K1MC, * K2C1, K2MC, rep from * to end.

8th row: P1C1, * P2MC, P2C1, rep from * to end.

9th row: * K2C1, K2MC, rep from * to last st, K1C1.

10th row: * P2MC, P2C1, rep from * to last st, P1MC.

11th row: * K2MC, K2C1, rep from * to last st, K1MC.

12th row: * P2C1, P2MC, rep from * to last st, P1C1.

Change to 3.25 mm needles.

Using MC, work 2 rows st st.

Using C2, work 2 rows st st.

17th row: Using MC, as 1st row.

18th row: Purl.

19th row: Using C1, * sl 1, K1, psso, yfwd, rep from * to last st, K1.

20th row: Purl.

Using MC, work 2 rows st st.

Change to 3.75 mm needles.

23rd row: K3MC, * K7C2, K1MC, rep from * to last 2 sts, K2MC.

24th row: P4MC, * P5C2, P3MC, rep from * to last 9 sts, P5C2, P4MC.

25th row: K5MC, * K3C2, K5MC, rep from

* to end.

26th row: P6MC, * P1C2, P7MC, rep from * to last 7 sts, P1C2, P6MC.

Change to 3.25 mm needles.

Using MC, work 2 rows st st.

Using C1, work 2 rows st st.

31st row: Using MC, as 1st row.

32nd row: Purl.

33rd row: Using C2, as 19th row.

34th row: Purl.

Using MC, work 2 rows st st.

Change to 3.75 mm needles. **

Rep from ** to ** for patt.

Cont in patt until work measures 22(25,29) cm from beg, working last row on wrong side.

Shape shoulders

Keeping patt correct, cast off 7(9,10) sts at beg of next 4 rows, then 8(8,9) sts at beg of foll 2 rows.

Leave rem 25(25,27) sts on a stitch holder.

FRONT

Work as given for Back until there are 16(16,18) rows less then Back to shoulder shapings.

Shape neck

Next row: Patt 28(32,36), TURN.

*** Keeping patt correct, dec one st at neck edge in every row until 22(26,29) sts rem. Work 3(3,4) rows ***.

NOTE: This side of neck is shorter to accommodate shoulder band.

Shape shoulder

Keeping patt correct, cast off 7(9,10) sts at beg of next row and foll alt row.

Work 1 row.

Cast off.

MEASUREMENTS

To fit underarm	cm	41	46	51
	ins	16	18	20
Jumper				
Actual measurement				
	cm	46	51	56
Length to back neck				
	cm	23	26	30
Sleeve seam	cm	14	17	20
Leggings				
Outside leg length	cm	31	34	37

MATERIALS

Cleckheaton Babysoft 4 Ply (25 g) balls (or other suitable 4 ply): 3(3,4) balls Main Colour (MC — White), 2 balls 1st Contrast (C1 — Blue), 1 ball 2nd Contrast (C2 — Yellow) for Jumper; 5(5,6) balls C1 for Overalls; 1 pair each 2.75 mm (No. 12), 3.25 mm (No. 10) and 3.75 mm (No. 9) knitting needles or the required size to give correct tension; 2 stitch holders, 3 buttons for Jumper; length of round elastic, 2 buttons for Overalls.

TENSION

30 sts to 10 cm over st st, using 3.25 mm needles.

It is important to knit a tension square and to work to the stated tension in order to obtain the required measurements. If your square is bigger use finer needles. If your square is smaller use thicker needles.

Cuddly toys are always a special favourite and will continue to be much-loved for many years. Make this baby-sized teddy bear following the pattern and instructions on page 71. Choose a pretty printed cotton, velveteen or felt for the bear and stuff it with lightweight polyester fibre. Loose buttons and beads are very dangerous so always embroider or paint features on (with non-toxic paint) and make sure all ribbons and trims are very well secured.

Slip next 13 sts onto stitch holder and leave.

Join yarn to rem sts and patt to end.

Work as given from *** to ***.

Work 7 rows.

Shape shoulder
Complete as for other shoulder shaping.

SLEEVES
Using 2.75 mm needles and C1, cast on 37(37,39) sts.

Work in rib as given for lower band at Back, until band measures 3 cm from beg, ending with a 2nd row and inc 8 sts evenly across last row. 45(45,47) sts.

Change to 3.25 mm needles and MC.

Work in st st, inc one st at each end of 5th and foll alt rows until there are 51(55, 57) sts, then in foll 4th rows until there are 61(67,73) sts.

Cont without shaping until side edge measures 14(17,20) cm from beg, ending with a purl row.

Shape top
Cast off 5(5,6) sts at beg of next 8 rows.

Cast off rem sts.

NECKBAND
Using back stitch, join right shoulder seam. With right side facing, using 2.75 mm needles and C1, knit up 71(71,75) sts evenly around neck edge (including sts from stitch holders).

Work 7 rows rib as given for lower band of Back, beg with a 2nd row.

Cast off loosely in rib.

LEFT FRONT SHOULDER BAND
With right side facing, using 2.75 mm needles and C1, knit up 31(35,39) sts evenly along Left Front Shoulder and side edge of Neckband.

Work 3 rows rib as given for lower band of Back, beg with a 2nd row.

4th row: Rib3(4,6) [K2tog, yfwd, rib10(11,12)] twice, K2tog, yfwd, rib2(3,3). 3 buttonholes.

Work 3 rows rib.

Cast off loosely in rib.

LEFT BACK SHOULDER BAND
Work as given for Left Front Shoulder Band, omitting buttonholes.

TO MAKE UP
Press lightly on wrong side with a damp iron if desired. Overlap front shoulder band over back shoulder band and stitch in position at armhole edge.

Using back stitch, sew in sleeves, placing centre of sleeve to shoulder seams. Join side and sleeve seams. Sew on buttons.

OVERALLS
RIGHT LEG (beg at waist)

Using 2.75 mm needles and C1, cast on 81(85,89) sts.

1st row: K2, * P1, K1, rep from * to last st, K1.

2nd row: K1, * P1, K1, rep from * to end.

Rep 1st and 2nd rows until work measures 5 cm from beg, ending with a 2nd row and inc one st at end of last row. 82(86,90) sts.

Change to 3.25 mm needles.

Work 2 rows st st (1 row K, 1 row P).

Shape back
NOTE: To avoid holes when turning, bring yarn to front of work, slip next st onto right hand needle, yarn back, slip st back on to left hand needle, then turn and proceed as instructed. ****.

1st row: K14(16,18), turn.

2nd and alt rows: Purl.

3rd row: K21(23,25), turn.

5th row: K28(30,32), turn.

7th row: K35(37,39), turn.

9th row: K42(44,46), turn.

Cont turning in this manner, working 7

more sts in alt rows until the row "K70(72,74) turn" has been worked.

Next row: Purl.

***** Cont in st st, inc one st at each end of 11th and foll 10th(12th,14th) rows until there are 88(92,96) sts.

Cont without shaping until shorter edge measures 16(17,19) cm from beg, ending with a purl row.

Tie a coloured thread at end of last row to denote back edge.

Shape leg
Dec one st at each end of next row and foll 3rd rows until 58(66,86) sts rem, then in foll 4th row/s until 56(60,64) sts rem.

Cont in st st until side edge measures 15.5(17.5,19.5) cm from coloured thread, ending with a purl row and dec 13 sts evenly across last row. 43(47,51) sts.

Change to 2.75 mm needles.

Work 12 rows rib as given for waist.

Cast off loosely in rib. *****

LEFT LEG (beg at waist)
Work as given for Right Leg to ****.

1st and alt rows: Knit

2nd row: P14(16,18), turn.
4th row: P21(23,25), turn.
6th row: P28(30,32), turn.
8th row: P35(37,39), turn.
10th row: P42(44,46), turn.
Cont turning in this manner, working 7 sts more in alt rows until the row "P70(72,74), turn" has been worked.
Work as given from ***** to ***** noting to tie the coloured thread at beg of relevant row, instead of at the end.

BIB
Using back stitch, join centre front and centre back seams. Tie a coloured thread half way between centre front and centre back seams on each side.
With right side facing, using 3.25 mm needles and C1, beg 3 cm in from coloured thread, knit up 53(59,65) sts evenly to within 3 cm of other coloured thread.
1st row: K3, purl to last 3 sts, K3.
2nd row: Knit.

Rep 1st and 2nd rows until work measures 8(10,12) cm from beg, ending with a 2nd row.
Work 2 rows rib as given for lower band of Jumper.
Next row: Rib 8, yfwd, K2tog, rib to last 10 sts, K2tog, yfwd, rib 8.
Work 3 rows rib.
Cast off loosely in rib.
STRAPS (make two)
Using 2.75 mm needles and C1, cast on 17 sts.
Work in rib as given for lower band of Jumper, until strap measures 19(22,25) cm from beg, ending with a 2nd row.
Cast off loosely in rib.

TO MAKE UP
Using back stitch, join leg seams. Thread elastic through rows of rib at waist as desired. Sew straps in position to back of Overalls. Cross straps. Sew on buttons.

BLUE STRIPED OVERALLS

SIZE: 6 to 12 months

MATERIALS
- [ ] 1 m of 115 cm wide cotton
- [ ] 30 cm x 12 cm fusible interfacing for bib
- [ ] 4 mm narrow piping cord
- [ ] two 14 mm buttons
- [ ] 30 cm of 2 cm wide elastic

PATTERN
Pattern outline ▬ ▬ ▬ ▬ ▬
19 bib (cut 2); 20 front/back pants (cut 2)
Cut out pattern pieces as directed. 1 cm seams allowed. Join all pieces together with right sides facing. Trace leg facings as separate pieces off legs. Cut a 10 cm square for pocket and four pieces 50 cm x 4 cm for straps. Cut approximately 4 m x 4 cm of bias for piping and 10 cm x 4 cm bias for pocket facing. Cut a piece 29 cm x 8 cm for back casing.

1   Interface bib. Make piping.
2   With piping in between, and right sides together, sew facing to pocket top. Turn

facing to inside. Press and edgestitch. Press remaining raw edges of pocket to inside. Edgestitch into place.
3   Sew front and back crotch seams. Neaten and press. Sew inside leg seams. Neaten and press.
3   Sew side seams of leg facings. With piping in between, raw edges even and right sides together, sew facings around leg ends. Stitch through all thicknesses. Turn facings to inside. Press and edgestitch all around leg ends. Turn in raw edge of facings and stitch down onto pants legs. Turn cuffs to right side.

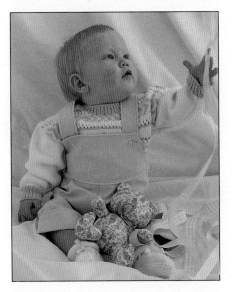

4   Fold pleats at front waist. Tack pleats into place. With raw edges matching, sew piping around waist.
5   With piping in between, raw edges even and right sides facing place bib and facing together. Stitch around curved top edge through all thicknesses. Turn and press. Edgestitch all around curved edge of bib.
6   With raw side edges matching, sew casing to bib as far as centre line of casing. With right sides facing, sew bib and casing to pants waist. Turn in 1 cm on raw edge of inner casing and stitch down over previous stitching. Thread elastic through casing, adjust length and secure ends at side seams with a double row of stitches. Press all raw edges towards bib. Turn in 1 cm on lower edge of bib facing. Slipstitch folded edge of facing over previous stitching. Edgestitch waist.
7   With piping in between, right sides facing and raw edges matching, sew both long sides and one curved short end of straps. Trim seam, turn and press. Position open end of straps, crossed over, on back casing. Trim ends and neaten diagonally to fit. Stitch securely into place. Edgestitch top of back casing over straps.
8   Make buttonholes. Sew on buttons.

Blue Striped Overalls, Fair Isle Jumper. Make the little floral teddy in exactly the same manner as the one on page 71.

JUMPER AND PANTS

BACK
Using 2.75 mm needles, cast on 69(75,83) sts.

1st row: K2, * P1, K1, rep from * to last st, K1.

2nd row: K1, * P1, K1, rep from * to end.
Rep 1st and 2nd rows until band measures 3 cm from beg, ending with a 2nd row.
Change to 3.25 mm needles.
Cont in purl fabric, (1 row P, 1 row K) until work measures 22(25,29) cm from beg, ending with a knit row.

Shape shoulders
Cast off 8(9,10) sts at beg of next 4 rows, then 8(8,9) sts at beg of foll 2 rows.
Leave rem 21(23,25) sts on a stitch holder.

FRONT
Using 2.75 mm needles, cast on 71(79,87) sts.
Cont in rib as for lower band of Back until band measures 3 cm from beg, ending with a 2nd row.
Change to 3.25 mm needles.

1st row: P19(23,27), K2tog, yfwd, K3, P23, K2tog, yfwd, K3, P19(23,27).

2nd row: K19(23,27), P5, K23, P5, K19(23,27).

3rd row: P19(23,27), K3, yfwd, K2tog, P11, Bobble, P11, K3, yfwd, K2tog, P19(23,27).

4th row: K19(23,27), P5, K11, P1tbl, K11, P5, K19(23,27).

5th row: P19(23,27), K2tog, yfwd, K3, P8, Bobble, P2, K1tbl, P2, Bobble, P8, K2tog, yfwd, K3, P19(23, 27).

6th row: K19(23,27), P5, K8, P1tbl, K2, P1, K2, P1tbl, K8, P5, K19(23, 27).

7th row: P19(23,27), K3, yfwd, K2tog, P6, Bobble, P1, FC, P1, K1B, P1, BC, P1, Bobble, P6, K3, yfwd, K2tog, P19(23,27).

8th row: K19(23,27), P5, K6, P1tbl, K2,(P1, K1) 3 times, K1, P1tbl, K6, P5, K19(23,27).

9th row: P19(23,27), K2tog, yfwd, K3, P6, FC, P1, FC, K1tbl, BC, P1, BC, P6, K2tog, yfwd, K3, P19(23,27).

10th row: K19(23,27), P5, K7, BC, K1, P3, K1, FC, K7, P5, K19(23,27).

11th row: P19(23,27), K3, yfwd, K2tog, P8, FC, Ml, sl1, K2tog, psso, Ml, BC, P8, K3, yfwd, K2tog, P19(23,27).

12th row: K19(23,27), P5, K9, BC, P1, FC, K9, P5, K19(23,27).

13th row: P19(23,27), K2tog, yfwd, K3, P9, purl into front and back of next st, sl1, K2tog, psso, purl into front and back of next st, P9, K2tog, yfwd, K3, P19(23,27).

14th row: K19(23,27), P5, K11, P1, K11, P5, K19(23,27).

15th row: P19(23,27), K3, yfwd, K2tog, P23, K3, yfwd, K2tog, P19 (23,27).

16th row: As 2nd row.
Rows 1 to 16 inclusive form patt.
Cont in patt until there are 16(18,18) rows less than Back to shoulder shaping.

Shape neck
Next row: Patt 28(32,35), turn.
** Keeping patt correct, dec one st at neck edge in foll alt rows until 24(26,29) sts rem.**
Work 1 row.
NOTE: This side of neck is 6 rows lower to accommodate Left Front Shoulder Band.

Shape shoulder
Keeping patt correct, cast off 8(9, 10) sts at beg of next row and foll alt row. Work 1 row. Cast off.
Slip next 15(15,17) sts onto a stitch holder and leave. Join yarn to rem sts and patt to end.
Rep from ** to **.
Work 8(6,6) rows.

Shape shoulder
Complete as for other shoulder.

SLEEVES
Using 2.75 mm needles, cast on 39(43,45) sts.
Cont in rib as for lower band of Back until band measures 3 cm from beg, ending with a 2nd row and inc 10 sts evenly across last row. 49(53,55) sts.
Change to 3.25 mm needles.

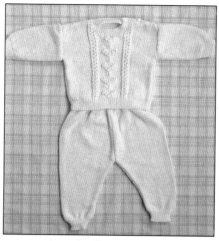

MEASUREMENTS
Jumper

To fit underarm	cm	41	46	51
	ins	16	18	20
Actual measurement				
	cm	45	50	55
Length to back neck				
	cm	23	26	30
Sleeve seam	cm	13	15	18
Leggings				
Outside leg length				
	cm	31	34	37

MATERIALS
Cleckheaton Babysoft 4 Ply (25 g) balls (or other suitable 4 ply): 5(5,6) balls for Jumper; 4(4,5) balls for Leggings; 1 pair each 3.25 mm (No. 10) and 2.75 mm (No. 12) knitting needles or the required size to give correct tension; 2 stitch holders; 3 buttons; a cable needle for Jumper; round elastic for Leggings.

TENSION
30 sts to 10 cm over st st, using 3.25 mm needles.
It is important to knit a tension square and to work to the stated tension in order to obtain the required measurements. If your square is bigger use finer needles. If your square is smaller use thicker needles.

ABBREVIATIONS
Bobble = [(K1, P1) twice, K1], all in next st, turn, P5, turn, K5, slip 2nd, 3rd, 4th and 5th sts over first st.
FC = Slip next st onto a cable needle, leave at front of work, P1, then K1 from cable needle.
BC = Slip next st onto a cable needle, leave at back of work, K1, then P1 from cable needle.
Ml = Pick up loop which lies between next st, place on left hand needle, purl into back of it.
K1B = Knit one below, knitting both loops at same time.

Cont in purl fabric, inc one st at each end of 3rd row and foll 4th(4th,6th) rows until there are 61(63,65) sts, **2nd and 3rd sizes only** - then in foll (6th, 8th) rows until there are (67,69) sts.
Cont without shaping until side edge measures 13(15,18) cm from beg, ending

with a knit row.
Shape top
Cast off 8(9,10) sts at beg of next 4 rows, then 9(10,9) sts at beg of foll 2 rows. Cast off rem sts.
NECKBAND
Using back stitch, join right shoulder seam. With right side facing, using 2.75 mm needles, beg at left front shoulder seam, knit up 69(75,79) sts evenly around neck edge (including sts from stitch holder).
Cont in rib as for lower band of Back (beg with a 2nd row) until band measures 2 cm from beg, ending with a 2nd row. Cast off loosely in rib.
LEFT FRONT SHOULDER BAND
With right side facing, using 2.75 mm needles, knit up 25(29,33) sts evenly along right front shoulder edge.
Work 1 row rib as for lower band of Back.
Next row: Rib 2, [cast off 2 sts, rib 7(9,11)] twice, cast off 2 sts, rib 3.
Next row: Rib 3 [cast on 2 sts, rib 7(9,11)] twice, cast on 2 sts, rib 2.
Work 2 rows rib. Cast off loosely in rib.
LEFT BACK SHOULDER BAND
Work as for Left Front Shoulder Band omitting buttonholes.

TO MAKE UP
Overlap Left Front Shoulder Band over Left Back Shoulder Band, and slip stitch together at side edge. Sew in sleeves placing centre of sleeves to shoulders. Sew on buttons.

LEGGINGS
RIGHT LEG (beg at waist).
Using 2.75 mm needles, cast on 81(85,89) sts.
1st row: K2, * P1, K1, rep from * to last st, K1.
2nd row: K1, * P1, K1, rep from * to end.
Rep 1st and 2nd rows twice, inc one st in centre of last row. 82(86,90) sts.
Change to 3.25 mm needles.
Work 2 rows st st (1 row K, 1 row P).
Shape back
NOTE: To avoid holes when turning, bring yarn to front of work, slip next st onto right hand needle, yarn back, slip st back onto left hand needle, then turn and proceed as instructed. ***
1st row: K14(16,18), turn.
2nd and alt rows: Purl.
3rd row: K21(23,25), turn.
5th row: K28(30,32), turn.
7th row: K35(37,39), turn.

9th row: K42(44,46), turn.
Cont turning in this manner, working 7 more sts in alt rows until the row "K70(72,74), turn" has been worked.
Next row: Purl.
***** Cont in st st, inc one st at each end of 11th and foll 10th(12th,14th) rows until there are 88(92,96) sts.
Cont until shorter edge measures 16(17,19) cm from beg, ending with a purl row.
Tie a coloured thread at end of last row to denote back edge.
Shape leg
Dec one st at each end of next and foll 3rd rows until 58(66,86) sts rem, then in foll 4th row/s until 56(60,64) sts rem.
Cont in st st until side edge measures 15.5(17.5,19.5) cm from coloured thread, ending with a purl row and dec 13 sts evenly across last row. 43(47,51) sts.
Change to 2.75 mm needles.

Work 12 rows rib as for waist.
Cast off loosely in rib.****
LEFT LEG (beg at waist)
Work as for Right Leg to ***
1st and alt rows: Knit.
2nd row: P14(16,18), turn.
4th row: P21(23,25), turn.
6th row: P28(30,32), turn.
8th row: P35(37,39), turn.
10th row: P42(44,46), turn.
Cont turning in this manner, working 7 sts more in alt rows until the row "P70(72,74), turn" has been worked.
Work as for Right Leg from **** to ****, noting to tie a coloured thread at beg of the relevant row, instead of at the end.

TO MAKE UP
Using back stitch, join back, front and leg seams. Thread round elastic through 1st, 3rd and 5th rows of rib at waist.

LEMON SCENTED BOOTEES

Using 3 mm needles, cast on 43 sts.
1st row: (K1, inc in next st, K18, inc in next st) twice, K1.
2nd and alt rows: Knit.
3rd row: (K1, inc in next st. K20, inc in next st) twice, K1.
5th row: (K1, inc in next st, K22, inc in next st) twice, K1.
7th row: (K1, inc in next st, K24, inc in next st) twice, K1.
9th row: (K1, inc in next st, K26, inc in next st) twice, K1.
11th row: (K1, inc in next st, K28, inc in

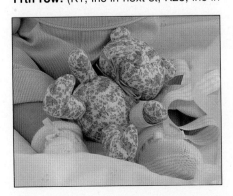

next st) twice, K1.
12th row: K2tog, K63, K2tog. 65 sts. ***
Work 10 rows st st (1 row K, 1 row P).
Shape instep.
Next row: K37, K2tog, turn.

MEASUREMENTS
To fit 0-6 months
NOTE: For slightly smaller bootees, use one size smaller needles than those which give correct tension. For slightly larger bootees, use one size larger needles than those which give correct tension.

MATERIALS
Cleckheaton Babysoft 3 Ply (25 g) balls (or other suitable 3 ply): 1 ball; 1 pair 3 mm (No. 11) knitting needles or the required size to give correct tension; about 85 cm of 6 mm wide ribbon.

TENSION
32 sts to to cm over st st, using 3 mm needles
It is important to knit a tension square and to work to the stated tension in order to obtain the required measurements. If your square is bigger use finer needles. If your square is smaller use thicker needles.

Next row: Sl1, K9, K2tog, turn.
Rep last row until 45 sts rem (17 sts on each side of instep).
Next row: K10, K2tog, then knit to end.
Next row: Purl. 44 sts.
Ankle
Next row: K1, * yfwd, K2tog, rep from * to last st, K1.

Next row: Purl, inc one st in centre. 45 sts.
Next row: K2, * P1, K1, rep from * to last st, K1.
Next row: K1, * P1, K1, rep from * to end. Rep last 2 rows 3 times.
Using C, work 14 rows garter st (every row K).
Cast off.

TO MAKE UP
Using a flat seam, join boot and back seam, reversing back seam above rib. Thread ribbon through eyelet holes and tie in a bow. Fold ankle section above rib to right side.

CARRY-ALL BAG

MATERIALS
☐ two pieces pre-quilted cotton 65 cm x 90 cm for inside and outside
☐ two pieces pre-quilted cotton 65 cm x 21 cm for inner pockets, two pieces pre-quilted cotton 50 cm x 36 cm for outer pockets
☐ two strips plain fabric 1.60 m x 12 cm for handles, two strips plain fabric 65 cm x 5 cm for inner pocket edging
☐ four pairs stick-on Velcro dots
☐ fusible interfacing

1 Sew edging strip to right side of one long edge of each inner pocket. Turn to wrong side and stitch to secure. Tack pockets along short sides of inner bag, matching raw edges. Stitch to divide pockets into three equal compartments.
2 Fold outer pockets over double with right sides together. Stitch along one long side only. Turn and press. Fold outer bag

over double with wrong sides together. Pin an outer pocket to centre of each outer side. Tack. Stitch across lower edge of

pocket.
3 Interface straps. Fold straps over double with right sides together. Stitch long sides. Turn and press. Join ends of each strap. Topstitch length of straps several times. Place straps around outer bag, with join at lower fold and edge of straps covering outer edge of pockets. Stitch both edges of straps to bag from top of one pocket, around bottom of bag to top of other pocket.
4 Make two ties about 40 cm long from fabric scraps. Pin to right side of centre top edge, with raw edges matching. Keeping straps and ties clear, place inner and outer bag together with right sides facing and raw edges matching. Stitch around edge, leaving small opening for turning. Turn and press. Close opening by hand.
5 Open out bag and fold inner pockets towards centre. Close bag and mark and attach Velcro dots to inside top corners.
6 To use, open out bag and inner pockets and lay flat as shown. Lay nappy on top of centre section, if desired, before using as a changing pad.

LACE-TRIMMED SHEET AND PILLOW

MATERIALS
☐ 2 m of 115 cm wide cotton fabric
☐ 3.2 m cotton lace
☐ thin wadding

1 Make sheet in same manner as embroidered sheet on page 61, omitting embroidery and adding lace.
2 Generally it is best not to use a pillow for a very young baby, so we have chosen a flat pillow with no stuffing. To make pillow, trace around shape of bassinet and extend to about 35 cm in length. Cut out two pillow shapes in fabric and one in wadding, allowing 1 cm seams. Pin lace around curved edge of right side of one piece with raw edges even, folding in short ends of lace to neaten. Tack wadding to wrong side of trimmed piece.
3 Place back and front together with right sides facing. Stitch around edge, leaving small opening for turning. Turn and press. Close opening by hand.

HOW TO USE THIS BOOK

KNITTING AND CROCHET
MATERIALS

We have suggested the brand and ply of knitting yarn for each pattern. If changing knitting yarn from the one suggested, remember to knit a tension square.

ABBREVIATIONS

alt = alternate; **amt** = amount; **beg** = beginning; **ch** = chain; **comm** = commencing; **cont** = continue; **dc** = double crochet; **dec** = decrease; **dtr** = double treble; **fin** = finished; **foll** = following; **g st** = garter stitch; **htr** = half treble; **inc** = increase; **incl** = including; **k** = knit; **k2tog** = knit 2 together; **lhs** = left hand side; **lp** = loop; **meas** = measures; **p** = purl; **patt** = pattern; **psso** = pass slip stitch over; **rem** = remaining; **rep** = repeat; **rhs** = right hand side; **rnd** = round; **rsf** = right side facing; **rsr** = right side row; **sl** = slip; **sl 2tog** = slip 2 together; **sp** = space; **st/s** = stitch/es; **st st** = stocking stitch; **tbl** = through back of loop; **tr** = treble; **wsf** = wrong side facing; **wsr** = wrong side row; **yfwd** = yarn forward; **yrh** = yarn round hook; **yon** = yarn on needle

TENSION

The correct tension is given for each pattern. It is important to work to the correct tension to ensure a properly fitting garment. Read the information about tension on page 21 before you begin knitting.

MEASUREMENTS

The sizes of knitted garments are given as actual measurements rather than by age. Remember babies of the same age can vary considerably in size, so trust your tape measure and if possible take fresh measurements just before you begin knitting each garment.

TO MAKE UP

Take care to assemble your garments neatly for a professional finish. Plain knitting usually looks best if the pieces are pressed on the wrong side, using a warm iron and a damp cloth. Some yarns and textured knitting should not be pressed so check the ball band and pattern instructions carefully. Seams on patterned or multi-coloured knitting are usually best pinned first, to ensure that patterns and colours match up. Use back stitch for joining pieces unless otherwise stated.

SEWING
PATTERNS

The patterns for most of the designs in this book are given full size on the pull-out pattern sheet. Each pattern piece for a particular garment has the same outline and this is shown at the beginning of the sewing instructions. We suggest you fix the pattern sheet to a firm backing, such as cardboard. Trace the pattern pieces off the sheet as you need them, using ordinary tracing paper from your newsagent or haberdasher. This way you will be able to go on using your pattern sheet for a long time. If there is a particular pattern you think you might use again and again, trace the pattern pieces onto non-woven interfacing. This will last much longer than tracing or tissue paper and can be labelled and kept without tearing or crumpling. When tracing off your pattern pieces remember to transfer all labels, instructions and markings as you go.

A few smaller patterns have been given full size. Simply trace these off and you're ready to go. The pattern for the little teddy bear on page 71 is drawn on a grid. You will need to draw up your own grid, where each square is 2.5 cm x 2.5 cm, and transfer the outline onto it. If you wish to enlarge the embroidery pattern on page 61, a photocopier will do that very effectively to any size you wish.

MATERIALS

Often a particular fabric has been suggested for a sewn item and this is the one we have pictured. Do not be restricted by our choices, but experiment with your own.

ACKNOWLEDGEMENTS

The Publishers of this book would like to thank the following people who assisted in the production of this book: Cleckheaton Yarns designed and produced the knits; Naomi Quiroz and Kate McEwen, from Kate McEwen's Sewing Centre, Chatswood and Sue McIver sewed the quilts; Offray provided the ribbons; XLN Fabrics; Canning Vale Towels and John Mazzolani provided the folk art. All the items were sewn on Bernina and Pfaff sewing machines.

KNITTING NEEDLES CONVERSION CHART

Metric (mm)	2.25	2.75	3	3.25	3.75	4
English	13	12	11	10	9	8
US	0	1	2	3	4	5